NOT OUT OF MIND

Prayer when a baby dies

NOT OUT OF MIND
Prayer when a baby dies

A collection of 21 liturgies
and useful resources
for Christian clergy and bereaved parents
to facilitate prayer when a baby dies
during pregnancy or around birth

By Althea Hayton

ARTHUR JAMES
BERKHAMSTED

First published in 1998 by

ARTHUR JAMES LTD
70 Cross Oak Road
Berkhamsted
Hertfordshire HP4 3HZ

A catalogue record for this book is available
from the British Library.

ISBN 0 85305 441 X

Typeset in Baskerville by Watermark
Cromer NR27 9HL

Printed in Great Britain by
The Guernsey Press Co. Ltd.
Guernsey

*This book is dedicated
to all parents bereaved in the past and in years to come,
and to those who care for and minister to them.*

This book was made possible by the creativity and generosity of hundreds of people, too numerous to mention individually, including members of clergy, lay church workers, nurses and medical staff, parents and the staff of voluntary organisations. The hidden grief of bereaved parents, denied for far too long, has provided the fuel for the Not Out Of Mind project, which I have co-ordinated since 1991 and which gave rise to this book. My task has been to collate and disseminate the stories and liturgical material that have arrived on my desk unbidden. With this book the task is now completed.

Contents

PART TWO: EXTRA RESOURCES

Introduction

Just as you do not know the way of the wind or the mysteries of a woman with child, no more can you know the work of God who is behind it all. ECCLESIASTES 11:5 (JB)

A parent's experience of pregnancy is not always a positive one: there are times when the tender hopes of parenthood are dashed by the premature ending of a pregnancy and the consequent death of the baby.

The Christian response to such a tragedy has until recently been woefully inadequate. The existing manuals of prayer and liturgy hold little material suitable for use when a baby dies, and even the training of our priests fails to address adequately the theological issues involved.

This book is intended to fill the gap that is experienced when clergy, parents, bereavement workers and other professionals look to the Christian faith to bring some meaning to an event that turns our normal expectations upside down – the death of a baby before birth.

The theological questions that arise go to the heart of our Christian traditions. There is the issue of when or whether to baptise, and there is the question of whether a miscarried or aborted foetus should receive a funeral. How can anyone give comfort to a woman who had felt the first stirrings of life in her womb only to be told by an ultrasound radiologist that the heart has stopped and that the baby's brief life is now over?

Is this woman truly a mother? Was her unborn baby a

separate person with a soul? Where is her baby now? This book can only hint at some of the questions, rather than provide answers, for there are none to be found, other than to trust in the infinite mercy of God.

New liturgies

It is through the willing and extensive provision of appropriate prayers and liturgy that the Christian church can provide a caring response to tragedy. Suffering bereaved people have always turned to prayer in their despair, both within their own faith and through their local church.

At last the Christian churches are beginning to address this long-neglected area of need among their parishioners. Many of those enlightened clergy have contributed their ideas to this book.

The right to mourn

Having been for too long hidden and unacknowledged, pregnancy loss is now recognised as a true bereavement. Some 36% of conceptions are lost before birth, so this represents an enormous ongoing need, not to mention the pent-up grief of previous generations of women denied the right to mourn their dead children.

In the wake of the feminist revolution, mothers are beginning to demand the right to grieve openly. As the clamour increases, the sheer numbers involved will become overwhelming. Public baby bereavement services of prayer, often involving many hundreds of grieving parents, can help to meet this need.

The death of a baby touches almost every family, and the whole community can be affected by the stark sadness of a pregnancy that ends in death instead of new life. Grieving parents who find no solace in the church at the time of their greatest need can become isolated from both faith and church. If clergy can reach out with liturgy and we can all be willing to come together in prayer, then we can create a greater sense of community and a more trusting faith.

PART ONE

A COLLECTION OF LITURGIES

1

Baptism and its Alternatives

Do not be afraid, for I have redeemed you;
I have called you by your name, you are mine. ISAIAH 43:1 (JB)

This chapter is intended to address a familiar dilemma for hospital chaplains, that is, when and whether to baptise a very sick, dying or dead baby. Three liturgies are detailed below:

☆ A baptism in emergency for a sick baby likely to die very soon.

☆ A service of blessing and naming for a child born dead.

☆ A service of baptismal desire for bereaved parents.

═══

A NEONATAL DEATH:
BAPTISM IN EMERGENCY

Hospital chaplains are often asked by staff to baptise a baby in imminent danger of death. Their reaction is likely to vary with their individual theological position. For example, such a situation can create a real dilemma for priests who have been trained to believe that there is a need for the parents to demonstrate something of their own faith before giving baptism to their child. There may be no time for such a discussion, and distraught parents, watching their tiny baby lose the struggle to live, can hardly be questioned.

The chaplain may have to go ahead with the baptism and waive this requirement in order to carry it out at all. The very fact that they had asked for the chaplain could, under the circumstances, be considered the equivalent of saying 'I turn to Christ'.[1]

There are two principal attitudes to the baptism of the dying newborn: one suggests that without baptism there can be no salvation, and the other affirms the infinite mercy of God and the innocent purity of the newborn. Baptists dedicate children; consequently, anxious parents may be refused baptism. After 'hands on' experience, a new chaplain may change his view.[2] As is often the case, the practice drives the theology, and very few chaplains will refuse baptism to a distraught parent. Even if there is a feeling that a liturgy of baptism will make little theological sense, the meaning for the parents is enormous. Many hospital chaplains see this issue as a pastoral rather than a theological one.[3]

The request for emergency baptism is an important moment for a parent: it is at one time an acknowledgement that the baby's life is in danger, yet it is also an expression of the fact that a new tiny person has come, however briefly, into the world.

The form of prayer is less important than the fact that the minister is allowing God to work through him or her. The experience of baptising a newborn baby can bring the feeling that God has again become a baby with such dreadful vulnerability.

Through baptism the new baby can be acknowledged and named by the world and created a new Christian in God's name. Most parents feel that baptism ensures a place in heaven for their child, despite the fact that any mention of limbo as a place for the innocent unbaptised has long gone from theological discussion. For Christian parents and families the idea of a baby dying unbaptised can be distressing.

Note: If there is no priest available and time is short, parents or staff who are themselves baptised Christians may baptise the baby. This is done by applying the water and saying the baptism prayers given below. If this happens, parents should inform the chaplain later so a baptism certificate can be given and the baptism recorded.

MODEL LITURGY[4]

☆ The officiant may wear a white stole.

☆ Some water may be warmed slightly in a small vessel, such as a shell, or tiny bowl reserved for the purpose or provided by the parents.

☆ A little cotton wool will also be needed.

☆ The officiant asks for the **name** of the child.

☆ Everyone makes a sign of the cross, if this is desired.

☆ A little warmed water is dripped over the baby's head with the cotton wool as the priest says the **baptism prayer**:

> N., I baptise you in the name of the Father, the Son and the Holy Spirit. Amen.

☆ The following may be included if time allows:

☆ Before the baptism a **welcoming prayer** by the officiant:

> Lord God Almighty, ever mindful of the weak among us: this baby is so small, but he/she is made in your image. Be with us as we prepare to welcome this new baby into the life of your Spirit.[5]

☆ A **short sentence** from the Bible, e.g. Mark 10:14–15.

☆ A **thanksgiving prayer** by officiant after baptism:

> God our Father, for the gift of this new life, the love of these parents and the fellowship of the Holy Spirit, we give you thanks. Send forth your grace upon N. &

N., that this child may know their love always, and grow in the knowledge that you are with us today and for ever, even until the ending of the world.

Blessing (17d)*

Note: If the baby dies during or immediately after baptism the priest may still be present, and can (with the parents' permission) offer a short prayer commending the baby to the love of God. (10b)

======

A STILLBIRTH IN HOSPITAL: A SERVICE OF BLESSING AND NAMING

In the last ten years it has become normal practice for a mother and father to see and hold their stillborn baby. The time spent with the baby's body may create a need for some kind of prayerful acknowledgement of their child's brief life in the womb. Calling for a chaplain, they may ask for the baby to be baptised.

A parent's request for baptism of a dead baby may not be as meaningless as it seems: baptism is the only common form of prayer that is associated with the birth of a baby. Sadly, there is no other form of prayer commonly used to welcome babies into the world.

Unfortunately, when a baby is born dead, there is no possibility of baptism. Baptism is for the living, not the dead, but this stark observation is hard to make to Christian parents faced with the still body of their beloved child. However, a sensitive minister can pre-empt any request for baptism by offering a service of naming and blessing.

---

* Numbers in brackets refer to the prayers in chapter 11.

The parents of a child born dead can never know this baby, and neither can any siblings born or yet to be born. The naming fixes the child in history and acknowledges its separate existence. Now that stillborn children are registered, the name is also used on official documents relating to the baby. Most importantly the baby can be prayed for and referred to by name, so where possible, the name for the child should be included in the liturgy. As there is no baptism certificate to keep, a specially made blessing card with the name of the baby, plus date and the name of the minister, can be handed to the parents afterwards as a token of the event.

The blessing emphasises the closeness of the baby to God, being totally innocent. The blessing of the baby can come to symbolise the sanctity of a life only ever experienced by the mother, kicking in her womb, and perhaps seen moving by the family on the screen of the ultrasonic scan.

This new life, ending at birth, is not to be thrown away as useless but granted a special spiritual status by being blessed. The blessing bestows on the event some kind of meaning, encompassing the tragedy in the grand scene of creation. This little life can now be seen as blessed – as deeply loved by God as any baby that thrives and lives to be old.

The use of oils can bring some hope to the parents, who are aware of their child's suffering and are in need of healing themselves. This is how the strength and comfort of God can be felt as very near, sharing the pain and upholding them in despair.

MODEL LITURGY

Before the service

✩ When meeting the parents the minister may say:

> If your baby had lived I expect you would have wanted him to be baptised. Would you like me to name your baby and to bless him? When Jesus died he was anointed with oil. If you would like me to do so I can anoint your baby with oil and mark him with the sign of the Cross.

✩ The officiant may wear a white stole.

✩ The officiant will need oils, a candle, a white cloth and a blessing card.

✩ The baby may be wrapped in the white cloth, or the cloth laid over the baby's body.

✩ The mother may wish to hold the baby, or it may be left in the basket or cot.

✩ A candle may be lit as a potent symbol of life in the midst of death, and may be kept as a souvenir. Meanwhile, the officiant may say a prayer (6b).

✩ The officiant may ask for the name of the child.

✩ The officiant may offer a naming prayer:

> Lord God, you knew us all by name before time began. In the sure knowledge of your love for all creation, we give this baby the name N.

Note: If the name has a special meaning, a prayer may be said in the hope that the quality suggested by the name will live on in the family. If a saint's name is given, a reference to the saint may be made, e.g. 'St Monica pray for us.'

Blessing the child

✩ With the oils a sign of the Cross may be made on the child's forehead or bare chest.

✩ The officiant offers a prayer as this is done.

> Heavenly Father, you anointed your Son, Jesus Christ, with the Holy Spirit and the power to bring us all to the blessings of your kingdom. I now anoint N. with the same Holy Spirit, that we who are sharing in this suffering may bear witness to the gospel of salvation, through Christ our Lord. Amen.

Blessing

✩ The officiant may offer a blessing, such as:

> May the blessing of God be upon you and the love of God be with you, now and always.

Prayers for healing

✩ A parent may say 13c – a prayer asking for healing.

✩ The officiant may offer the parents an anointing for the healing of hurts.

Prayer for peace

✩ This prayer (9a) may be accompanied by a sign of peace between those assembled. In this way, however divided the people present may be in their beliefs, they are united in praying for the baby.

Final blessing

✩ The officiant may give a blessing for all those present. (17b)

A card

✩ A special card may be created and signed by the

officiant and handed to the parents as a souvenir in the absence of a baptism certificate. As an example, it might have a Bible quotation such as Isaiah 49:16 as an inscription on the front. On the card might be written words such as:

> In loving memory of N. We had looked forward to welcoming you into our family. May you now be welcomed into the kingdom of God's love and enjoy for ever the glorious liberty of the children of God.

> Anointed and named. (Date: name of hospital)

=====

SERVICE OF BAPTISMAL DESIRE FOR BEREAVED PARENTS[8]

It can happen that the parents of a stillborn child have spoken to a priest of their intent to baptise the child before it was known that the baby would die. In these circumstances it may be hard for the parents to leave aside the matter of baptism.

This liturgy demonstrates that when a baby dies there are so many times when the usual prayer books just do not meet the need. Those who listen sensitively to the needs of bereaved parents can find a way to resolve the terrible bewilderment that stillbirth can bring, with the thought that 'everything has been done right' for the baby.

MODEL LITURGY[9]

Welcome

✴ The officiant may give a few words to welcome the parents and acknowledge the sadness of the situation.

Introductory prayer

✫ The officiant may say:

It is the church's understanding that not even a sparrow shall fall outside the knowledge and love of God our Father. And the concern of Jesus for children is one of the striking moments of St Mark's Gospel.

✫ The officiant may read Mark 10:13–16.

✫ The officiant may continue:

Yet in the frailty of our minds, the mysteries of life and death are hidden from us. It is therefore necessary and right, on such an occasion as this, to show both our sadness and our trust. So let us speak to God, in thought and prayer and action.

✫ Here the officiant may light a candle and hold it during the following prayer and hand it to the parent(s) before the second prayer.

Prayer of desire for baptism

✫ The officiant may say:

Lord Jesus, we have followed your command and sought baptism for this our dearly loved child N. In the mystery of your will his/her life returns to you. May our desire that he/she should be a member of your body (the church) be granted.

May this candle symbolise your light in our saddened lives, and his/her incorporation into the body of your faithful people who with the Father and the Holy Spirit draw us all to your everlasting life. Amen.

✫ The officiant may now hand the candle to the parents.

Prayer for the parents

✫ The officiant may offer a prayer for the parents (12g).

The Lord's Prayer

☆ The officiant may introduce this prayer with the words:

> Let us commend ourselves and our loved one(s) to God, in the words our Saviour gave us:
> Our Father . . .

Final prayer

☆ The Grace or the Gloria may be said. As these are very well known prayers, they may be spoken by everyone present, showing the shared desire for baptism.

☆ The candle may be given as a token of the event.

☆ The card of naming and blessing may be signed by the minister and handed to the parents to keep.

━━━

Let the little children come to me, and do not hinder them, for the kingdom of heaven belongs to such as these. MARK 10:14 (NIV)

2

Baby Funerals

Blessed are those who mourn, for they will be comforted. MATTHEW
5:4 (NIV)

This chapter gives details of four special funeral services:

☆ for a stillborn baby in a church;

☆ for a stillborn baby at the graveside;

☆ for a miscarried baby;

☆ for a baby aborted on grounds of abnormality.

═══

A FUNERAL FOR A STILLBORN BABY

A generation ago it was usual for a stillborn baby to be
taken away immediately after birth and for the mother not
to be given sight of it. Perhaps the father may have seen it,
but rarely would the mother. In those days, not so long
ago, the body of the baby would be taken by the authorities
and buried with an adult in a communal grave, or perhaps
in a country churchyard under the hedge. The idea was
'out of sight, out of mind'; but we now know that these
babies were never out of mind and were silently remembered, always with love and sorrow, by their mothers and
fathers.[1]

The idea of 'getting the baby out of the way so as not to

distress the parents' still lurks in the corners of the funeral profession, and perhaps explains why we still hear of mothers of stillborn babies, barely out of bed and hardly able to stand, swaying numbly in a chill graveyard, unable to think or feel.[2]

The rush to disposal

If the mother of the child is still very ill after the birth – perhaps having had a Caesarean delivery and needing to recuperate – it may be possible for the funeral of the baby to be delayed by a week or so. In making a decision like this there are two factors to weigh in the balance: on one side there is the need for the mother to be well enough to attend the service, while on the other there is a sense that until the funeral is over the grieving cannot begin.

It is a mistake to equate the death of a baby at birth with any other kind of death. Stillbirth is the death of a brand new person, who is not yet known to the world. There should be no haste to dispose of such a person until the existence of this new baby can be fully appreciated by the parents. Time to hold, wash, dress and simply be with their new baby is vital for the parents to be given some sense that there ever was a real baby at all.[3]

Stillbirth is possibly the most difficult of losses to bear. A new baby, snatched away by death at the very moment of birth, is transformed into a cold, waxen-faced object 'to be disposed of as soon as possible'. It is an insult to the feelings of the parents, and the short but not insignificant life of that child, not to allow time to let the parents recover sufficiently to take some interest in the funeral. However, the nature of grief is such that the family is likely to be stunned and incapable of making decisions, and they are likely to fall in with the wishes of any significant professional.[4]

A minister of religion can have some influence in slowing down the progress towards disposal in order to give love a chance to grow and be expressed. After a normal birth there can be a gradual process of greeting the newborn, and creating the parental bond with the child – a process of saying 'hallo'. This is not available to the parents in the case of stillbirth. A blessing and naming ceremony can help (see p. 20), as can the chance to be with the child as much as possible. Only when the introductions have been made will everyone be ready to say goodbye.[5]

Choices, not decisions

There are some cases where the parents are ready, willing and able to create a funeral service almost by themselves.[6] For the most part however, the parents, in the first stages of shock and numbness, will welcome some guidance. They are not likely to be able to decide for themselves what they would like for a prayer or song. However, they may be able to choose between two or three given alternatives. In the service suggestions set out below I have given three choices where possible, which might give the parents choice and provide variety for the minister concerned.

Remembrance

Stillbirth is so tragic that even the most appropriate funeral will become little more than a vague painful memory for the parents. A memorial service – perhaps to mark the first anniversary of the baby's death – can give full expression to the parents' desire to remember their child with their full involvement.[7] A model liturgy for this kind of service is given in Chapter 4.

A compromise is to hold a funeral service in the parish church, after which the family may leave for the burial. This may be very hard on the parents, as they would be involved in two services in the same day, but more people can be invited and the whole parish can be seen to be mourning with the family.

The best funeral

In my view, there are three main considerations when creating a funeral for a stillborn child: brevity, pertinence and sincerity. The funeral of a stillborn child is no time for long prayers or homilies; the parents can only bear so much. Yet if things are too brief, that may not do justice to the loss.

Simply adapting the normal funeral liturgy is not enough. The thoughts and prayers must be pertinent to the loss. In this case the tragedy is that Hallo becomes Goodbye; there is anger and bewilderment at God and there are questions with no answers.

To be at all meaningful, the funeral of a stillborn child must be a highly emotional experience for all, and that includes the minister. Parents are comforted if their loss is seen to touch other people outside the family, because it shows that people truly care.[8]

Dealing with feelings

Allowing sincerity while maintaining dignity is an almost impossible balance to maintain: it is too easy to harden one's heart in order to cope with the feelings engendered by the death of a tiny baby.[9] Self-control is of course needed in abundance in this situation, but perhaps the words spoken and the tone of voice used can convey some of the feelings we all share as a result of such a tragedy.

It is a good idea if, wherever possible, clergy debrief one another after holding a funeral of a baby or child. The open expression of feelings and the outpouring of suppressed tears need not be done alone and in private, but can be and should be shared with the support of a friend or colleague.

It is possible for all professionals involved with the death of a baby to find a way to integrate this kind of loss into their lives, but without good support this is unlikely to happen.[10]

A LITURGY IN CHURCH BEFORE THE COMMITTAL[11]

Mementoes of the brief life of the baby, with photographs and some toys, may be set out for the congregation to see. A specially created card or book may be signed by all those attending, which can help to make memories of the baby. There are three suggestions given for some elements of the service. This may allow parents to make a choice.

☆ The people gather.

Welcome prayer

☆ The priest or minister may say a few informal words (or 1f).

Bible reading

☆ The officiant or a deacon may read one of the following:
    Psalm 25:4–7, 17, 20 (Lord, let me know your ways)
    Ecclesiastes 11:5 (the way of the wind)
    Isaiah 61:1–2 (to comfort the mourning)

Prose/poetry reading

☆ A member of the family may read one of the following:
    *R33: A lily of a day
    R9: Still born
    R8: For a child born dead

Song

☆ The people may sing one of the following:
    We cannot measure how you heal (see p. 131)
    Fleetingly known (see p. 130)
    Hymn based on Isaiah 49 (see *Hymns Old and New* (Kevin Mayhew, 1989), no. 265)

Readings

☆ A lay person may read one of the following:
    R14: Footprints
    R29: A little thing
    R7: Life within

---

*'R' numbers refer to readings in Chapter 12

Tribute to the baby

☆ A member of the family may read their own tribute or R10.

Song

☆ The people may sing one of the following:
Psalm 23 (The Lord's my shepherd)
Be still and know that I am God
Lord of all hopefulness

Prayers for the family

☆ The officiant may say one or more of the following prayers:
12e – for the baby's parents.
12n – for the baby's brothers and/or sisters.
12o – for the baby's grandparents.

Blessing

☆ The officiant may give 17f – a blessing.

Music

☆ Some instrumental music may be played as the family leaves for the burial/cremation (see Chapter 10).

AT THE GRAVESIDE OR CREMATORIUM

This liturgy is short and simple, showing our care for the needs of the bereaved while showing God's care for little children.[12]

Note: For convenience, the three choices of prayer are given in full so that the service may be taken directly from these pages.

Welcome prayer

☆ The officiant may say one of the following:

1j – N. & N., we come here today to commend baby N. to our heavenly Father, and to commit his/her body to be cremated; to assure you of the everlasting love of God, to share in your sorrow and to offer you comfort and support.

1e – May the peace, compassion and hope that is God be with you in this moment and in the days ahead.
And with you.
We are today in the face of severe loss. We are overwhelmed as we reflect upon the mystery of life and death. We pause silently as we reflect on this mystery, the pain of our grief and our love for baby N. and each other.

1f – We are gathered here at a very sad time. We were looking forward to a time of joy, and instead there is sorrow. Our feelings of loss and grief are hard to bear. It is hard to understand why baby N. has been taken from us. But there are truths which we can hold on to: God our Creator loves us all, and through his son, Jesus Christ, he has promised that he will not leave us or forsake us. Nothing in death nor life can separate us from his love.

Bible reading

☆ The officiant may read one or more of the following:
   Mark 10:13–16 (Let the children come)
   Psalm 139:13–16 (You created my inmost self)
   Isaiah 40:11 (Like a shepherd)

Prayers

☆ The officiant may say one of the following prayers:

   3i – God of Hope, we come to you in shock and grief and confusion of heart. Help us to find peace in the knowledge of your loving mercy to all your children, and give us light to guide us out of our darkness into the assurance of your love.

15b – Heavenly Father
your love for all children
is strong and enduring.
We were not able to know our baby (N.) as we hoped.
Yet our baby was known to you.
In the midst of our sadness
We thank you that N. is with you now.

15a – Lord of all life,
thank you for your prodigality,
for your work in creation,
for nourishing life in the womb,
for your love even in death.
Thank you for these brief lives
whom you gave us and have taken to yourself.
Thank you for the arms of your love, embracing us all in your family.
Thank you for your presence in our sorrow and your strength in our continuing lives.

Commendation

✻ The officiant may say one of the following:

10b – Into God's loving care and compassion, into the arms of that infinite mercy, we commend this baby/child N. May he/she share in the risen life of Jesus Christ, our Saviour.

10d – Father, help us to entrust this baby N. to your never failing care. We give back to you, our Heavenly Father, what you once gave to us; which was always yours and always will be. We believe that we are united with N. in your unending love, through Jesus Christ our Redeemer.

10e – Let us commend this baby to the Lord's merciful keeping; and let us pray with all our hearts for N. & N. Even as they grieve at the loss of their (little) child, they entrust him/her to the loving embrace of God.

The Lord's Prayer

☆ The people may say this together.

Committal

☆ The officiant may say one of the following prayers:

11e – Lord God, ever caring and gentle, we commit to you N., quickened to life for so short a time. Enfold him/her in your eternal life.

11d – We have now come to say our goodbyes to N., and as we have entrusted him/her into your hands, we now commit his/her earthly body to the elements. Ashes to ashes, dust to dust; having our whole trust and confidence in the mercy of our heavenly Father and in the victory of his Son, Jesus Christ our Lord, who died, was buried and rose again for us and is alive and reigns for ever and ever.

11g – Lord God, we return N. to you. As N. & N. grieve at the loss of their child, we entrust N. to your loving care.

Prayer for parents

☆ The officiant may say one of the following:

11f – God of life, death and eternity, we thank you for the gift of this baby N., and the blessing through tears he/she has brought us. Help us now to entrust him/her to your unfailing care and love. Transform our grief into new hope and bring us to the fullness and completeness of joy beyond our imagining.

12f – God our Creator, comfort this family, grieving for the loss of their hoped-for child. Help them to find reassurance that with you nothing is wasted or incomplete, and uphold them with your love, through Jesus Christ our Saviour.

12g – O Lord, whose ways are beyond understanding, listen to the prayers of your faithful people: that these weighed down with grief at the loss of this little child may find reassurance in your infinite goodness. We ask this through Jesus Christ our Lord, who lives and reigns with you and the Holy Spirit. Amen.

Blessing

✫ The officiant may say one of the following blessings:

17e – May Christ the good shepherd enfold you with love, fill you with peace and lead you in hope, this day and always.

17c – May the love of God and the peace of the Lord Jesus Christ console you and gently wipe every tear from your eye.

17f – O Lord, help us to remember that you care for us, and that in your will is our peace. And may the Lord Jesus Christ be with you to defend you, within you to keep you, before you to lead you and above you to bless you.

═══

A FUNERAL AFTER A MISCARRIAGE

A Roman Catholic mother,[13] who miscarried in hospital in the late 1980s, asked that the tiny body of her ten-week-old baby be collected and placed in a jar. This she took home and wished to place in the family grave. A priest was asked to say a prayer at the graveside. This was asked for in the belief that the body deserved the same treatment as the larger body of another of her children, miscarried at 14 weeks and buried in the same grave two years before. On neither occasion did the priest refuse to pray.

In contrast to this, a young Roman Catholic mother[14] who miscarried a baby at 20 weeks in hospital in the early 1970s went to her priest for some prayer of comfort. She was told that the miscarriage was a 'punishment for her sins' and was refused any kind of prayer or service. The hurt engendered by this experience poisoned her relationship with the Church for decades. It is to be hoped that the practice of offering prayers after miscarriage is beginning to overturn this unfortunate attitude.

Dignified disposal

In the early 1990s, it was highlighted by the SANDS group that the bodies of babies miscarried in hospital were disposed of along in the hospital incinerator with other hospital waste. This was held to be not in keeping with their human status, and a directive was sent out that all miscarried babies should be disposed of in a dignified manner.[15]

Some babies are miscarried entire but some are removed surgically in a womb evacuation operation and as such are not fit to be seen. If miscarried entire, the baby's body may be shown to the mother if she wishes it. A 20-week baby is large enough to wrap in a shawl and be cuddled. These later miscarried babies, though they are not registered as births, are real children to their parents – particularly if they have been seen and touched.

It is now much more common for funeral directors to be asked to create funerals for tiny miscarried babies (non-viable foetuses) of less than 24 weeks of gestation. Some professionals believe that this is not helpful to the parents, because it may magnify a miscarriage from an unfortunate loss into a tragedy and might increase the bewilderment that is experienced at such a time.[16] However, only a small proportion of mothers and fathers of miscarried babies ask for a full-scale funeral, and it is my belief that only those who truly need it ask for it. Providing the option gives the right to choose.

How do I pray?

Some kind of prayer is said at the committal of the bodies of miscarried babies, wherever they are disposed of, and whether the parents are there or not. (See Chapter 3.) But how should we pray at a funeral for a baby miscarried at, say, 20 weeks?

A funeral commits the body to the earth or to dust, and a Christian funeral offers the soul of the departed into the hands of God. If the miscarried baby is prayed over in this way, then that implies a belief in the spirit of that tiny little person being able to share in eternity.

The concept of limbo, once a popular belief to encompass this eventuality, has now passed out of use, and indeed some prayers suggest that the parents and the child will meet again,[17] which is a statement of faith that indeed the child is not condemned to limbo but, being perfect, is able to see God. With that in mind, the funeral service for a stillborn child given above may be used, with the following exceptions:

3b – a parent's prayer
12g – prayer for parents
10d – prayer of commendation
11e – committal prayer
16g – final prayer

====

A FUNERAL AFTER AN ABORTION ON GROUNDS OF ABNORMALITY

In the many funeral liturgies I have been shown for this project, I have detected no difference in the beliefs expressed in the prayers, be the funeral for a stillbirth, a miscarriage or an abortion on grounds of foetal abnormality.

The belief behind the prayers of the funeral service for a stillborn baby is that the spirit of that baby will live on – that the baby will in some sense see God. Those who would advocate that the life of an unborn baby be ended for reasons of abnormality should perhaps be aware of those implications. In 1991 it was thought by some that offering a funeral service after abortion for abnormality may imply that the parents had killed their child. This attitude no longer seems to prevail.[18]

Distraught parents

Parents who made the decision to go forward with the operation often seem to have experienced some ambivalence about the decision, and a great deal of heartache.[19] If a Christian person has ambivalent feelings about a decision, clearly there will be some soul-searching and feelings of guilt – maybe not at first, when the trauma of the event causes a numbing of all feelings, but later, when there is time to reflect.[20]

The double bind

When asked to say funeral prayers over the body of a baby aborted on grounds of abnormality, the Christian minister may feel caught in a double bind: his theology may show him that the decision to end the life of the child is against the teaching of the church, but he must in all humanity minister to the parents in their distress. He may be concerned that, if he gives sympathy, support and kindness in his pastoral care, and prays that God will comfort them in their grief, he may seem to be condoning the action.[21] If he does not minister to the parents he will be viewed as callous, inhuman and indeed, un-Christian. Weighing the two opposites in the balance, it seems to me that most clergy decide that, even where an action is against the teachings of the church, the person who took that action needs help, love and support.

A *stage further*

I am afraid that it often happens that in the case of abortion on grounds of abnormality the pastoral care stops when the funeral is ended. I believe that there is a further stage that can be taken. This is not at the funeral, but later when the parents begin to recover from the trauma. In love and kindness the minister can help the parents to finally admit to themselves that ending their baby's life went against the teachings of the Christian church.

This is not to inflict guilt upon already distressed people, but to allow full expression of denied feelings of guilt. If this guilt is acknowledged, lovingly accepted and given expression in the knowledge of the forgiveness and mercy of God, then in this way the Christian church can bring healing and real comfort.

The need to pray after abortion

Just after the baby dies is obviously not the time for such a process, for the parents are likely to be very vulnerable at that time. However, the ambivalent feelings of the parents might be implied in the funeral service. With the word 'distress' instead of praying for comfort, the minister may express the hope that the parents will find a path to healing and peace.

If the Christian church were seen to be offering regular special services for parents after abortion,[22] then ministers saying the funeral prayers would not be thought to be condoning the action that occasioned the funeral. Simply, an aborted baby has as much spiritual value to God as any miscarried foetus, and deserves as much prayer. The pastoral needs of the parents may be seen as quite separate from this.

MODEL LITURGY

Note: It is suggested that this service be brief, while addressing all the issues.

✧ The people gather.

Welcome

✧ The officiant may say:

> 1j. N. & N., we have come here today to commend your son/daughter N. to the love of God, to commit his/her body to be cremated, to share in your distress and offer you our prayers and support.

Sentences from scripture

✧ The officiant may read one or more of the following:
> Wisdom 4:8 (on the length of life)
> Isaiah 43:1–2 (you are mine)
> Matthew 10:29 (the fall of a sparrow)
> Mark 10:14 (let the children come)

Psalm

This is to reflect the parents' feelings of numbness and need for help from God. A short extract may be read to keep the service brief. It is suggested that all present read it aloud. It may be arranged with responses, or spoken as a canticle.

✧ All may read aloud one or more of the following extracts from scripture:
> Psalm 25:4–5 (a wish to know the ways of God)
> Psalm 61: 1–3 (hear my cry)
> Psalm 130:1–2 (a cry out of the depths)

Bible reading

✫ A lay person may read from the New Testament, emphasising the comfort and hope of the resurrection.
Matthew 5:4 (the beatitudes)
John 6: 37–40 (I will raise it up on the last day)
John 14:1–6 (many rooms in my Father's house)

An address

There may be a place here for the officiant to address the parents and all present about the mixed feelings there must be in every heart on such an occasion; the love of God for all his children, as shown in the Gospels; and the infinite mercy of God, as described in the Psalms.

Prayer

✫ The officiant may say 12e – a prayer for the parents.

Silent meditation

✫ A period of silence may follow.

The commendation

✫ The officiant may say 10d – a prayer commending the baby into the hands of God.

The Lord's Prayer

✫ All join together in this prayer.

Prayers of committal

✫ The officiant may say the following:
11g – a prayer emphasising God's love for the child.
14a – a prayer of letting go.

Blessing

✫ The officiant may say 17f – a blessing.

After the service

Some days or weeks later, the family may appreciate a pastoral visit. At that time it may be possible to open the door to the parents to return to the church for some further prayer at a later date, should they need it. If special services are normal practice in the parish, this may be an opportunity to mention that a service of memorial and healing after abortion will be held at a later date, and to contact them with an invitation.

———

Length of days is not what makes age honourable, nor number of years the true measure of life. . . . WISDOM 4:8 (JB)

3

Alternative Rites of Committal

Before I formed you in the womb I knew you;
before you came to birth I consecrated you . . . JEREMIAH 1:5 (JB)

This chapter suggests four new model liturgies of committal that may be useful to clergy and parents when a baby dies but there is no body to be buried or cremated.

* The committal for cremation of non-viable foetuses in a hospital incinerator.

* The interment of ashes from the bodies of miscarried and aborted foetuses in hospital grounds.

* Disposal of the womb contents following a miscarriage at home.

* A service of committal for babies stillborn or miscarried some years ago, and disposed of without benefit of a funeral.

A RITE FOR USE BY HOSPITAL CHAPLAINS AT THE CREMATION OF NON-VIABLE FOETUSES

It is becoming increasingly common for hospital chaplains to be asked to commit for cremation the bodies of non-viable foetuses of between 10 and 24 weeks that have died within the last month or so. Regulations concerning the disposal of foetal tissue are very varied, and disposal methods vary enormously,[1] but whatever the local arrangements, chaplains are being placed in the situation of conducting some kind of service of prayer and committal for these babies.

This is a complex situation: the parents may not ask what is to happen to their baby's body, but in all fairness and good practice they should be consulted.[2] During this consultation, hospital staff should make clear that a Christian chaplain will be performing this duty, and that parents have a right to be there. This is very difficult in the case of abortion, and hospital practices vary enormously in this regard, which is understandable. However, if dignified disposal is to be a universal policy for non-viable foetuses, the issue of parental consent to disposal after abortion will one day have to be faced.[3]

If the parents are not Christian, it may be necessary to include some kind of prayer that allows for that fact, in particular for Jewish parents. They may be prepared to say their own prayer if they attend. Experience appears to be that very few parents attend, but this may change as the provision of this service becomes better known.

This kind of service of committal is an attempt to encompass the complexities of what may be a multi-faith/no-faith situation. The expressions of faith that lie behind the service (the love of God, the possibility of life after death and the support God gives to those who suffer) are common to most world religions, and hopefully a service of this nature would not offend anyone of a different faith, while allowing the chaplain himself to avoid compromising his own beliefs.

The parents have a right to be there, and if they are, their presence can be acknowledged.

MODEL LITURGY[4]

☆ Equipment needed may include:
  – a large candle;
  – a small stand or table, on which the casket stands, covered with a white cloth;
  – a posy of flowers provided by parents.
The parents may also like to bring a small candle or nightlight.

☆ The people gather in the hospital chapel. The large candle is lit, the smaller candle(s) lit from it as required by each parent.

Greeting (or if alone, a reflection aloud)

☆ The officiant may say:

My sisters and brothers, we/I come here today to commit these unborn children to the love of God which has neither beginning nor end. (From the Christian tradition) We understand this love to be beyond anything we can imagine in its compassion for the human race and its concern for the whole created order.

Bible readings

☆ Any person present may read:
  Psalm 42:1–3, 11 (why so downcast?)
  Matthew 13:1–7, 9 (the parable of the sower)
  Ephesians 3:17b–18 (Paul's blessing)

A period of silence

☆ Some quiet organ music may be played.

A selection of prayers may now be said

☆ The officiant may say 15a – a prayer of thanksgiving for creation.

☆ A parent may say 3b – a prayer for parents (if they are present).

☆ The officiant may say 12d – a prayer for the mothers of the babies.

☆ The officiant may say 12m – a prayer for the parents.

☆ All those present may say **the Lord's Prayer** together.

Song

Fleetingly known (see p. 130)

Thanks

☆ Any parent present may say 11f – a prayer of thankfulness for the brief life of their child.

Committal

☆ The officiant may say:

And so we commit these unborn children to be cremated. Ashes to ashes, dust to dust, confident that, in God, nothing is rejected or wasted, but that Christ is all in all.

Blessing

☆ The officiant may say 17d – a blessing to all those present.

☆ The candle is extinguished.

☆ The posy of flowers may be taken home by the parents

or left in the hospital chapel.

☆ Parents may like to leave the small candle burning, or to take it home for a souvenir.

═══

INTERMENT OF ASHES
AT A HOSPITAL[5]

As an alternative to the above liturgy, it can be made normal practice for hospitals to retrieve and keep the ashes of miscarried babies, cremated by the hospital in the absence of the parents, for a certain period of time (e.g., three months). Two or three times a year, the parents of these babies may be invited back to the hospital for a service of interment of ashes.

The following or similar reflections may be written on the service leaflet:

> Today we share in an act of closure; the final physical completion of a journey focused in the act of committing your baby's last remains to the earth. This service is an acknowledgement of the life of a person – your baby who has died, not a pregnancy that failed. In this way we acknowledge that you don't ever say goodbye in one day and at one service – you spend a lifetime saying goodbye.

> *You left a scar that will not pass, but I gladly pay the toll.*
> (From a father's poem for his baby)

MODEL LITURGY

The names of the miscarried babies may be given to the chaplain, to be read out during the service. These names may be held in a register for later perusal.

☆ The people may gather in the hospital chapel.

✫ The party may proceed to the hospital memorial garden where a small area of grass has been cut back to reveal bare earth.

✫ Some posies of flowers may be placed nearby, brought by the parents.

Welcome

✫ The officiant may say:

> We have come here today to commend our unborn and very prematurely born babies to our loving Creator God; and to commit their ashes to the earth.

Bible readings

✫ The officiant may read one or more of the following:
  Wisdom 4:8 (JB) (the length of life)
  Isaiah 40:1 (comfort my people)
  Isaiah 49:15 (the baby at the breast)

Prayer of commendation

✫ The officiant may say:

> Loving Creator God, Father and Mother of us all, be with us as we face the mystery of life and death. We come to you with all that has been part of the special gift of our babies; the joyful anticipation, the pain of love, of birth and death, of reaching out and letting go. Be close to us, heal us and give us courage and confidence as we commend them into the fullness of life that is your eternal presence. Amen.

Bible readings

✫ A lay person may read one or more of the following:
  1 Corinthians 13:4–13 (on love)
  2 Corinthians 1:3–5 (on comfort)
  Ephesians 3:14–21 (comforting blessing)
  1 John 3:1–2 (we are children of God)

Address

☆ The officiant may give a short reflection that may include:

The hello that becomes a goodbye
The need to make memories for tomorrow
There are no answers when we ask 'Why?'

Prayers

☆ The officiant may say one or more of the following prayers:

15a – in thanks for the brief lives of the babies.
12e – for the families.

Commendation

☆ A lay person may read out the names of the babies.

☆ The officiant may say:

Into God's loving care and compassion
Into the arms of infinite love and peace
We commend these our unborn and prematurely
    newborn babies,
in the assurance that they share unending love.

The committal

☆ The officiant may sprinkle some ash onto the bare earth, saying:

We entrust our babies into God's merciful keeping.
We commit their ashes to their final resting place.

☆ Parents may join in as ashes are sprinkled into the ground.

Closing prayer

☆ The officiant may say:

God of comfort,

We thank you for all that has been part of the gift of
our babies –
For those who have shared the difficult journey with
us;
For those who have given strength, support and
comfort;
For those who have allowed us to simply 'be'.
We pray for all those like ourselves who have
experienced the death of a baby;
those experiencing infertility; those whose babies are
in neonatal units;
and those who lovingly care for them as agents of
your healing strength and wholeness.
Hear our prayers, through Jesus Christ our Lord.
Amen.

The Lord's Prayer

☆ As they recite this prayer, the group may like to join
hands around the patch of earth in a gesture of shared
loss, or couples may simply like to hold hands with each
other.

Blessing

☆ The officiant may say 17b – a final blessing.

PRAYERS AFTER A MISCARRIAGE AT HOME

A miscarriage at home can be a distressing, uncomfortable
and embarrassing experience. The presence of other children in the house can make it particularly difficult to be
open about it. Miscarriage often takes place in the toilet in
total privacy, and some women never mention to anyone
the fact that they were ever pregnant.[6]

There is a need to enhance understanding of how prayer can help to bring meaning to such an experience. It is to be hoped that the idea of prayer during and immediately after miscarriage may gradually spread as a habit, and those who may be in attendance at the time or shortly after may suggest that a prayer be made.[7]

SUGGESTED PRAYERS

✫ The mother may say a prayer for strength:

> Please, God, be with me at this time. I cannot hold my baby within me any more and it is time for me to let him go into your care.

✫ The mother may say a prayer in anger:

> O God, I am tested almost beyond endurance! I long to be mother to this child and this is not to be. I cannot understand how such a fragile little life should end so soon! I cannot feel your love and care for me and my baby. O God, you seem so far away, please hold me!

✫ The mother may say a prayer of penitence:

> I feel as if it is my fault, that I didn't do more to keep him safe. If it is my fault that my baby has died, please forgive me.

✫ The mother may say a prayer of sorrow:

> My baby is dead and part of me has died with him. I have an empty space inside where my baby was growing that is full of tears. There is a terrible silence there. Please, God, come into the silence and be with me.

A RITE OF DISPOSAL

Sadly, there are far too many women who have to live with the thought that they threw their miscarried baby into the dustbin or flushed it into the public sewers.[8] In the first few weeks of pregnancy the body of the baby is almost indistinguishable from the placenta, and there is a great deal of blood.

If the mother can bear to rescue the body of the baby – probably still in the amniotic sac – then she can set about arranging a fitting method of disposal. It is also helpful for mothers to see that the baby is perfect, and indeed to realise that there was in fact a baby.[9]

This extremely detached, realistic view may seem improbable to some, but it is through being realistic that women cope best: denial is one of the least helpful coping mechanisms when a baby dies during pregnancy.[10] Almost universally, the way through the grieving process and onward to acceptance of the loss begins with facing the truth. Where that truth has been denied for many years, the first step can be hard to take, so why not take it directly, when the baby has just been miscarried?

The methods of disposal at home are limited: the sewers and the dustbin are of course options available, but traditionally the bodies of our loved dead are either buried or burned. The tiny body (or a package of the total womb contents expelled) may be wrapped in paper and burned carefully on a small bonfire in the garden. The ashes, when cool, may be spread over the soil to mix with the earth. Alternatively the tiny body (or the total womb contents) may be buried in the garden. It is wise to ensure that they are wrapped and buried at least two feet deep, or they may be dug up again by dogs or rodents. The site may become a planting place for a small tree or shrub. There are no public health regulations governing the burial of miscarried babies in a private garden, as long as the pregnancy was less than 24 weeks in duration.[11]

SUGGESTED PRAYER

✩ The mother or father may say:

> O God, please bless us, because our baby has died. We are empty and sorrowful but we trust in your mercy. May our baby live in our memory as pure gift, and live in your presence for ever. Amen.

———

A FUNERAL LITURGY FOR STILLBORN AND MISCARRIED BABIES DISPOSED OF LONG AGO WITHOUT A FUNERAL

Until the 1980s, and in some areas even later, it was not considered usual, or even proper, to mark the burial of a miscarried or stillborn baby by a funeral service. At the time it was felt that a funeral would be too upsetting for the mother, who would not have been shown the body of her baby for the same reason. The baby was disposed of in any convenient way, which often meant in an adult coffin in a communal grave. The parents, denied the chance to participate in a ritual of committal and letting go, were expected to put the event behind them. The painful and unresolved grief for these babies may have remained hidden for many years.

Today the situation is very different.[12] Clergy of all Christian denominations are becoming increasingly familiar with the experience of being asked to say funeral prayers for a stillborn or miscarried baby. This leaves the parents whose babies died in pregnancy long ago with a sense of 'unfinished business'. They lost a baby but the atmosphere at the time did not encourage grieving, whereas now it is considered normal to grieve over pregnancy loss. Some of these parents are finding the courage to approach their local priest or minister and ask for the funeral service that they were denied to be held at last. The healing benefit of these services can be enormous, and it is to be hoped that their courage in coming forward is rewarded in a meaningful way.

The funeral service for a stillborn baby can be adapted for this occasion, but there are several important points to be grasped about this special liturgy, probably held many years after the event.

Naming

First, there needs to be emphasis on the fact that the child always existed as a distinct person. This can be hard if a name was never given at the time because it was not common practice.[13] There may have to be some preparation by the parents as they decide if they want to give the baby a name or not. Often, a deep feeling of the baby as a distinct personality does remain, and giving a name is easy – there may even be a name already.

If this is not so, it may be hurtful to put pressure on parents to name their baby in a hurry, and for Mr and Mrs Smith for example, the baby could simply be called 'Baby Smith'.

Feelings

The parents may not realise just how hurt they have been by the experience until they have a chance to express their anger in a special funeral liturgy.

They will need 'permission' to grieve. This is important, as for many grief will have been hidden from both family members and friends for many, many years, and the habit of denial must now be broken.

Parents will need to face the guilt that comes from not having grieved before, at least openly. There may also be guilt that they had abandoned their child because they do not know where the baby is. They may want to 'find' the baby by locating where the baby was interred.[14]

Where to hold the service

For some, a service at the place of interment can be helpful if this is known. If not a service in a church or in the churchyard involving the dedication of a plant or plaque to the baby's memory can be very moving.[15]

Questions

Parents and other family members may be facing spiritual issues such as, 'Why did God allow this to happen?', 'Where is my baby now?' or 'Will I meet my baby again?'[16] Hopefully the prayers will address these questions, even if the answer is that there are no answers, so that it can be seen as normal for bereaved parents to wonder in this way.

Ideally, the funeral liturgy should be adapted to the family's own understanding of what has happened to their child and the personal picture of heaven that they share. Readings that the family themselves have provided can be helpful.

MODEL LITURGY

Welcome

☆ The officiant may say a prayer to acknowledge the long journey that has been endured to reach this day, and the faith and courage shown by the parents:

> Welcome to this simple service in which we will remember that day . . . years ago, when N. & N. knew that their baby (N.) had died. A long time has passed until today, but the sense of sadness and loss is still as deep.
>
> Let us pray:

Spirit of God, strengthen in all of us the same faith in

the mercy of God that brought N. & N. here today. As we give thanks to you for the brief life of baby N., we pray that, by handing him/her into the arms of the Lord, the deep hurts that remain may be healed at last.

Bible readings

☆ The officiant may read one or more of the following:
Psalm 139:13–16 (you created my inmost self)
Jeremiah 31:15–17 (mothers weeping)

The parents' story

☆ The parents may like to tell the story of the birth and death of their baby, and how they decided to create this liturgy in the name of their child.

A reading from Susan Hill's *Family* may be used as an alternative.

Naming

☆ The parents may say 7a – a prayer to name the baby.

Penitence

Parents may for years have been angry at those who stopped them from seeing their child and being involved in the ceremonies of parting. This anger may have been exacerbated recently as social attitudes have changed.

☆ The parents may say 5c – a prayer of penitence.

Prayer of sorrow

☆ Both parents may say 2e – taking verses in turn, demonstrating that their loss is mutual.

Reading

☆ A parent may read R11 – Little Lives.

The long waiting time is now over, and the parents are ready to let go of the child into the love of God.

Letting go

☆ The officiant may say 10b – a prayer commending the baby/ies to God.

☆ The parents may want to lay a posy of flowers in a chosen place as a ritual of letting go.

Bible reading

☆ One of those present may read Romans 8: 38–39 (The love of God).

Final prayer

☆ The officiant may say 16c – a final prayer.

This prayer acknowledges that we can trust in the infinite mercy of God, and know that the babies are safe in his eternal care.

Blessing

☆ The officiant may say 17g – a blessing.

———

Peace I leave with you; my peace I give you. I do not give to you as the world gives. JOHN 14:27 (NIV)

4

Prayer and Healing

Yahweh, my God, I cried to you for help, and you have healed me.
PSALM 30:2 (JB)

This chapter provides three model liturgies for parents who have been deeply hurt by the loss of a pregnancy.

* Healing after the loss of a pregnancy.

* Memorial and healing for a childless couple after repeated pregnancy loss.

* Healing and memorial after termination of pregnancy for any reason.

═══

HEALING AFTER MISCARRIAGE[1]

The provision of this healing rite for parents after miscarriage may be resisted at first by the parents, if the baby's body is being held in the mortuary pending disposal. In this case the need for prayer may be focused upon the baby. Parents may feel they want to wait until the baby is disposed of and then they can look to their own need for healing. If this is so, then the liturgy can be delayed until they are ready.

The following or similar words may be included on the service sheet:

The experience of miscarriage is intense, the grief overwhelming and the hospital stay very short.

The emotional impact of miscarriage may be misunderstood by others, because there are no physical reminders of the event. Although the mother never forgets, for others the event is easily put to one side and forgotten.

Even the parents may find it hard to talk about it, and they can become divided by their grief. So to the normal feelings of loss and vulnerability are added feelings of hurt and anger at those who do not understand the meaning of this loss.

In the midst of these feelings there comes a search for meaning: why was a little new life created by God only to be snatched away before birth? The following liturgy uses imagery through language, tangible symbols and action. These can convey meaning based on our Christian faith, and give expression to the mystery of the love of God, present amongst life's bruises.

This liturgy is ideally used as soon as possible following the loss – probably in the same place as the delivery. The inclusion of other family members is encouraged, especially as sharing the rite will change the perceptions of what has been lost. If the gender of the baby has been clearly determined or if the parents have chosen a name, this assists the ritual.

MODEL LITURGY

Introduction

A small candle, representing the light of Christ in the darkness of shattered hopes, is placed, unlit, alongside a small bowl of scented oil, preferably with a few flowers floating on top; plus one long-stemmed flower, such as a rose, preferably in bud.

✩ Where possible background music is played.

✶ The people gather.

Welcome

✶ The officiant may say 1h – a prayer of welcome.

Silence

✶ A short time of silence is kept.

Responsorial prayer

✶ The officiant may say a responsorial prayer such as:

> We hold close the moment.
> *For we shall always live by remembering.*
> Delivering, nurturing God, as a mother is tender towards her children, so you are tender towards your children. In your mysterious silence and presence we acknowledge our silent hopes for the life/lives of this/these infant(s), who never spoke a word, cried, smiled, or walked this earth. Infant life, blessed be your memory.
> *Blessed be the womb that bore you.*
> *Amen.*

Bible reading

✶ A parent may read one of the following:
   Psalm 139:13–18 (You created my inmost self)
   Isaiah 43:1–3 (You are mine)
   John 14:1–4 (I leave you peace)
   Romans 8:38–39 (Neither life nor death)

✶ A parent may read one or more of the following:
   The prayer of St Paul[2]
   R27 – The Unfinisheds

Address

✶ The officiant may give a short homily or reflection.

The ritual action

⋆ The candle may be lit as a sign of the life of Christ within the darkness of death.

⋆ The officiant may introduce the use of oil as a tangible sign of inner healing and peace.

⋆ The officiant may say:

> We acknowledge that life is a gift from God conceived and growing within N.
> Bonding in love and warmth, you were filled with developing life.
> Today you feel a hole in the centre of your being – we too feel your void, we taste your suffering.
> With you we acknowledge the one who knew you in the womb, before the one who knew us in the womb.

⋆ The officiant may say to the people:

> I invite you to enter with me into the healing that God offers.

Anointing

⋆ The officiant takes the fragrant oil and anoints the palms of the mother's and father's hands together, saying:

> I will not forget you! See, I have engraved you on the palms of my hands. (Isaiah 49:15b–16a (NIV))

⋆ All present may anoint one another using the above or their own words.

Silence

⋆ A period of silence is kept. Music may be played.

Concluding prayer

⋆ The officiant may say a final prayer:

Holy God, strong Father, nursing Mother,
Jesus, Christ of God, through whom we are sons and
daughters,
reach within us and bring to birth
strength for today and hope for tomorrow.
Hold us in the cradle of your love.
Spirit of God, soothing balm of heaven, may the loss
of childbearing not limit your God-bearing presence
within the sanctuary of our lives. Amen.

Blessing

✩ The officiant may say 17g – a blessing.

━━

HEALING FOR A CHILDLESS COUPLE

In the case of a very early miscarriage there can be no funeral service to make real the life of this child, unknown to the world but yet so precious to its parents, particularly if the couple as yet have no living children. Also, one should not ignore the losses involved in infertility treatment, especially IVF, where each tiny embryo is a new life, planted in the womb but unable to stay.

As there is no visible sign to the public of there ever having been a pregnancy, it is possible for the childless woman to be misunderstood as one who does not want a child, or who is infertile. For her sake and for her husband every pregnancy loss must be acknowledged. It cannot be known if a woman who loses a baby in pregnancy will ever be able to bear a living child, and may have to live out her life grieving and childless.

These losses can be addressed with the help of prayer and memorial ritual.[3] For example a woman from Ireland, aged 60, wrote to me to tell me that she had recently asked for and been granted a special private liturgy. She had miscarried six times over the last twenty years and has no living children. In the liturgy she named each of her precious babies and gave them to God. At last, she feels at peace.[4]

Reminders

For parents who have nothing by which to remember the child, the service can create concrete reminders of the pregnancy and brief life of their child. It is helpful if objects such as candles, cards, flowers, poems, letters, artifacts, toys, etc., can be used in the liturgy.

The parents may want to write down some of the events that took place at the time of the pregnancy, that can fix the life of the child in time (for example, if the family moved house or bought a puppy) and may want to include their writing in the liturgy. A little casket or box can be made into which some of these objects can be placed, and which can be buried or burned as part of a ritual of letting go, in an echo of the funeral service.

The following liturgy model may also be followed by two parents in a small private devotion in their local church.

MODEL LITURGY[5]

☆ The people gather. Each couple is given a flower to hold.

☆ A candle is lit on a table in the centre of the circle, or if this is a church, on the altar.

Opening remarks

☆ The officiant may make an informal speech of welcome, to reflect the surroundings and explain the reason for the liturgy, which is to enable the couple present to let go of their memories and dreams and find peace of mind.

The mother's prayer

☆ The mother may like to write a short piece to read out.

An alternative prayer may be:

> Lord Jesus, you promised that the heavy laden may find rest in you. I bring before you today the many losses I have endured in my search for a baby: the loss of my tiny babies; of motherhood, of womanhood; of personal privacy and joy in my marriage.
>
> When Gabriel appeared to Mary, she said 'Thy will be done.' May I share in a little of the faith and strength she showed in that moment. As I remember in love the baby/ies I held within me for such a short time, be near me, and help me to find that peace of mind that only you can bring.

The father's prayer

☆ The father may wish to write a short piece of his own to read out. An alternative prayer may be:

> Our loving Father in heaven, I bring to you my longing for a child of my own, for the chance to share in your work of creation. May my faith in you bring me courage to face whatever the future holds, the strength to endure all the uncertainties of life. I ask you to uphold both of us over the coming months, and help us towards accepting your will in all things.

Psalm

☆ A parent may read Psalm 42:1–5 (thirsting for the Lord)

Bible reading

☆ A parent may read Matthew 10:29 (the fall of a sparrow)

The parents' prayers

☆ A mother may say 15a – a prayer of thanks for the brief unborn lives.

☆ A father may say the following prayer of trust in the mercy of God:

Lord God Almighty, we place all our hope in you. There is so much we do not understand. Help us towards a knowledge of your plan for us, and to trust in your infinite mercy.

Prayers for special needs

The officiant or the parents themselves may say one or more of the following:

☆ For a childless couple still trying for a family after repeated miscarriage:

God our Father, you have given us the chance to share in your work of creation, but again and again you test us by taking our babies back to yourself. In your mercy, grant us the faith to know your love for all things, and the grace to let your will be done.

☆ For an older woman after persistent miscarriage with no further chance to have children:

Lord God Almighty, you created the world and all things in it. For a short time after I conceived my children I was transformed into a mother. I am grieving the loss of my babies and the chance to be the mother of a living child. Please send me so much faith that I can keep believing in your mercy, so much hope that I may remember the brief lives of my babies, and so much love that I can use my mothering to bring happiness to the children of other women.

☆ For a woman whose husband died before the miscarriage occurred:

O God our heavenly Father, your servant N. died never knowing his child, who lived so briefly and who now has returned to you. Grant that as his wife N. grieves for him and remembers him in love, she may be comforted by knowing that all her loved ones are with you.

* For a woman who miscarries after special infertility treatment:

> God of mercy, look down on this woman who held for such a short time the promise of new life. May she know that you create nothing in vain and love all you have made. Uphold her in this troubled time and send her comfort in the knowledge of your love for all creation.

Placing the candles

* A candle can be lit for each baby to be remembered, and placed on a stand or table.

* If the liturgy is being held outside, a flower may be placed in the chosen spot.

* If the babies can be spoken of by name, so much the better, but it may not seem appropriate to give a name to a child miscarried very early in pregnancy.

Laying the flowers

* Each couple in turn come to lay their flowers among the candles.

* The officiant may say:

> Heavenly Father, by your mighty power you gave us life, and in your love you have given us a new life in Christ Jesus. With these flowers, we remember the tiny new lives these women carried for so short a time. As they lay these flowers close to the light of your presence, may each one of them feel able to lay down the memories of the babies they never saw and their hopes and dreams of parenthood. We ask this in the name of Christ our Lord, Amen.[6]

Psalm

✶ The following may be read or sung:
   Psalm 42:11 (why so full of heaviness?)

Letting go

✶ All those present may say the following:

> Almighty Father, Creator of all that is good, we entrust into your eternal care the children we may not keep. We hand over to you our dreams and troubles, our hopes of parenthood. We place our lives in your hands. Gently guide us through the years ahead, and renew our lives in your service. Amen.

Prayer for healing

✶ A parent may say 13b – the wounded healer.

Anointing

✶ The officiant may offer all those who wish it anointing for the healing of hurts.

✶ Each person in turn may approach the officiant, who will establish their particular hurt, and then anoint them.

Song

✶ While anointing is taking place, a song may be sung:
   'Be still and know that I am God.'

Final prayer

✶ The officiant may say 16f – a final prayer.

Blessing

✶ The officiant may say 17g – a blessing.

Final remarks

Each individual present may need to come again to similar

services, as healing for such deep hurt may take a very long time.

====

PRAYER AFTER ABORTION

As the grief associated with pregnancy loss is discussed more and more openly, those who have terminated a pregnancy are coming forward in greater numbers asking for prayer after the event. Men and women who have decided to terminate a pregnancy on the grounds that the baby was likely to be abnormal may decide upon a funeral. (See Chapter 2.)

Parents who some time ago decided to end a pregnancy but wish to remember their baby may attend a baby memorial service (see Chapter 5) alongside those whose pregnancies ended naturally. However, such services are not structured to meet their specific needs, and in my view it may be better to provide prayer specifically for women after abortion. I have set out below an explanation of the needs of women after abortion, with a description of how these needs may be met in a special rite of memorial, penitence and healing.

The feelings of women after abortion

There is a feeling of relief that the pregnancy is stopped and there will not be a baby to worry about. Some women say they feel relieved of an enormous burden.

The abortion may have to be kept secret. There may be little or no support from home or partner. There is a feeling that there is no one else in the world who understands. For some the experience is traumatic. The woman may be angry with the people who advised her to have the abortion and with those who felt it was something she should not be doing, along with those who should have been supportive but walked away and left them with the responsibility.

It may be hard for a woman after an early abortion, when she has never even seen a scan, to think of the loss as a baby. Following the event, she may realise she has been selfish or naïve. She may wish to undo what has been done; to bring the baby back; to make another decision. She may yearn for a baby to hold. This may be shown in a wish to be forgiven and to make a new start. She may feel she is of no value to herself or to others. This may be reflected in a loss of faith and a sense that she is not worthy of God's love.

What prayer after abortion can do

By attending a liturgy a woman can make the secret public, let go of the child and the pain and find a place to leave the burden. Liturgy can recreate a sense of relationship with others and with God; let her reach out and find someone ready to respond, and incorporate what has happened to her into what she believes.

The provision of liturgy can create a climate of acceptance and unconditional love; voice the truth and allow people to admit their own spiritual needs. Providing a rite of healing can help people to bring their brokenness, feelings of helplessness and pain, and to help them find new hope and a new way of being.

Liturgy can give people space and time to deal with the feelings and problems the abortion has brought. It can help combat a feeling of pointlessness in life and a prevailing sense of unworthiness and depression, and encourage a belief that change is possible, and that one can grow in understanding. There will be someone alongside on the journey to wholeness who has patience and will let things happen at their own pace.

Through prayer, a woman can repent and feel forgiven, and be able to forgive herself and others. She can acknowledge the true nature of the life and death of the child, the need to mourn for that loss, and the knowledge that the baby has a real existence beyond life.

MODEL LITURGY

Note: The liturgy model that follows is based upon a special liturgy created and held in 1996 in Hertfordshire, England, at a day conference on the needs of women after abortion.[7]

✰ Equipment may include several small candles, circles of paper and pencils, a white cloth and a centrepiece of flowers with a large candle, unlit.

✰ The room may be laid out with a circle of chairs. (A circle is holding and inclusive, but rows of seats may enable more personal privacy.)

✰ The people gather in silence while some soft instrumental music is played.

✰ The people may sing: 'Stay here, keep watch with me, watch and pray.' Taizé music.

A prayer of welcome

It is important that the welcome be genuine and the people feel accepted. The idea here is to indicate that God will take the burden from anyone who lets it go; that God is closest in the depths of despair; that God is always with us, whatever happens. This prayer can indicate that everyone, regardless of what they have done, can turn to God, who is waiting for them to reach out.

✰ The officiant may say:

I would like to welcome you all here today for this special liturgy. Each of us has come here today carrying a burden. For some of us it is sorrowful, for others it is angry. Some of us may have been feeling lonely and isolated. For each of you I hope this simple service of healing, prayer and memorial will bring you closer to God. In this place and among the prayer, music and silence I hope you will feel able to lay your burden at the feet of Jesus, who died and rose again to save us.

A prayer for peace

✰ A deacon or lay person may say a prayer for peace, such as:

> We come in peace today to be with one another. Jesus brought us a peace that the world cannot bring: let us offer each other a sign of that peace.

✰ The people may join hands to sing a song at this point: 'Shalom'.

Prayers of sorrow and penitence

✰ The officiant may say 2f – a prayer for those who bring a burden of sadness related to the abortion.

✰ The people may say the following prayer:

> In our fear we forgot you, Lord
> in our panic we turned away –
> like Peter we denied you, Lord,
> again and again.
> You promised forgiveness to those who repent.
> We are truly sorry, Lord.
> Please make us worthy of your forgiveness.[8]

This prayer reminds us that God is specially concerned with sinners, and that repentance is the route to forgiveness. It can be written out in the printed liturgy so that anyone who wants to can say it as an act of contrition.

Bible reading

✰ The officiant may read one of the following:
> Isaiah 25:6–9 (destroy death)
> 1 John 1:9 (forgiveness)

Silence

✰ A period of silence and meditation follows.

✰ At the end of this period, prayer 8a may be said.

✢ If preferred, some quiet music may be played, such as:
  'Jesus remember me, when you come into your
      kingdom'
  Taizé music.

Prayers

✢ The officiant may say a prayer on behalf of all those
  present:

> Jesus, we remember that before you came into your
> kingdom you went through the darkest time you
> knew on earth. Today we have come here to consider
> some of the deepest, darkest feelings human beings
> can go through.
>
> We thank you for whatever experiences we may
> have had of brokenness and darkness that brought us
> here today. We thank you because you can transform
> everything, and you are calling us to go back into the
> darkness and to meet those people who are still there.
> It is time to feel in us the life, the love and the hope
> that we have received from you: the power of your
> resurrection shining into the darkness.
>
> We thank you because the light is always brighter in
> the darkness. We offer our lives and the rest of this
> day to you. Amen.[9]

Memorial for the babies

✢ The officiant may say 6b – a preliminary prayer while
  lighting the large candle to remind those present of the
  presence of God.

✢ One of those present may read
  Matthew 18:20 (where two or three are gathered)
  John 8:12 (the light of life)

✢ The people may write the name of the baby they wish to
  remember on a circle of paper, with a few thoughts.
  Some examples of these prayers may be:

A father's prayer
I wish things had been different and we had known each other. I give you to God.

A mother's prayer
I will never forget you – your name is carved on my heart. Please forgive me.

A grandmother's prayer
I never knew you, but I know the pain that is now in our family since you left us. Rest in the love of God.

A sibling's prayer
We never knew you as part of our family, but you will live for ever in our memory. May God keep you safe with him.

☆ As an alternative or in addition, they may take a night-light, one for each baby.

☆ A lay person may read R29 – a meditation on the fact that God loves all creation.

☆ The officiant may say 12k – for those babies aborted on grounds of abnormality.

☆ Each person may light a nightlight and place it in the centre of the circle, or place the circle, folded to enclose the writing, into a small basket.

Prayer for parents

☆ The officiant may say:

Heavenly Father,
you are the giver of life,
and you share with us
the care of the life that is given.
Into your hands we commit in trust the developing life that we have cut short.
Look in merciful judgement on the decision that we have made,

and assure us in all our uncertainty
that your love for us can never change. Amen.[10]

A period of silence is kept

Healing

The focus now moves to the parents and anyone present who seeks healing for themselves, or on behalf of another. These prayers are said while the little lights are burning in the centre of the room.

☆ The officiant may explain the use of oils and the procedure for anointing.

☆ The officiant may say:

Lord, we come here as broken people. With your healing touch, bless the people present here today. Grant them the healing gift of tears, and the relief of knowing that you will take the burden from anyone who offers it to you. Draw near to us, Lord, and let us experience your closeness in this anointing. Amen.

☆ The people may also like to offer prayers:
13c – for knowledge of God.
13d – for new strength.

☆ Each person who so wishes is anointed by a member of clergy, who may speak a few words to each one.

☆ A song can be sung while the anointing proceeds: e.g., 'Lay your hands gently upon us' (see Chapter 10).

Final prayers

☆ The officiant may say:

We thank you, Lord, for this time of sharing. Fill us with your Spirit as we leave this place, and may we experience your peace this day and every day.

Reading or Song

☆ All the people may say or sing together:
   13a – the prayer of St Francis.

Final blessing

☆ The officiant may say 17f – a blessing.

   Note: There may be some need for special support for the distressed. Trained counsellors may be needed to help some people deal with their feelings. This should be made available but not forced upon anyone.

   People may like to take their candles and their circles of paper home with them.

———

I waited patiently for the LORD;
   he turned to me and heard my cry.
He lifted me out of the slimy pit,
   out of the mud and mire;
he set my feet on a rock
   and gave me a firm place to stand.
He put a new song in my mouth,
   a hymn of praise to our God.

PSALM 40:1–3 (NIV)

5

Baby Memorial Services for Small Groups

For where two or three come together in my name, there am I with them. MATTHEW 18:20 (NIV)

This chapter provides model liturgies for two baby memorial services for small groups:

✫ A private service held at home for a single family group mourning a baby (possibly more than one) lost during pregnancy or around birth.

✫ A multidenominational service for small groups (10–40) held in a room or church hall.

═══

A PRIVATE PRAYER SERVICE HELD AT HOME

There may be some parents who do not want to pray openly immediately after a baby dies during pregnancy or at birth. They may find it hard to be involved in prayer of any kind if they are numbed by the experience, and may be traumatised and unwell. There is a need for a private prayer service for parents to use when they are with their baby, or several months later when the numbness wears off and the grieving can begin. It may become the starting point of a spiritual journey towards some kind of acceptance of their loss and an integration of the loss into their lives.[1]

Who will come?

This service is private to the parents, but they may want a member of the clergy to be present, who may be consulted about the format and asked to come and participate.

A question arises about the possible involvement of siblings. The general consensus of opinion is that siblings, however young, will have some knowledge of the impending birth and will realise that there has been a loss and there is a great deal of sorrow and unhappiness around. A service of prayer can enable the loss to be spoken of openly and also for the siblings to be directly involved, and express what may be a real feeling of loss of their own.[2]

Members of the wider family and the grandparents may appreciate the chance to be present, although too large a group in the home setting might be a little inhibiting.

Expressing creative energy

A pregnancy brought to an end prematurely can leave the would-be parents with a great deal of unexpressed creative energy. A home-made service of prayer allows the expression of that energy in the memory of their dead child.

According to the talents of those involved, parents may feel moved to create prayers, poetry, music, painting, sculpture, embroidery or patchwork in the name of the baby. They may plant a tree or lay out a portion of the garden. These creative endeavours are an important expression of their love for the child, and as such can be offered in prayer. The higher the level of participation and involvement, the more creative energy can be expressed, and the greater sense of satisfaction felt afterwards.

MODEL LITURGY

The prayers suggested in this model liturgy assume that only one baby has died, but this service may be suitable for a mother who has lost some or all of her babies from a multiple pregnancy.

☆ In the room a central space may be created with chairs or cushions around it in a circle.

☆ Any items that are associated with the pregnancy and birth of the baby (toys, bootees, wristband, appointment cards, photos etc.) may be displayed.

☆ Specially created items, such as a framed prayer or picture that includes the baby's name may also be placed centrally.

☆ Siblings or parents may want to make a decorated sign of the baby's name to place in the centre of the space.

☆ A large candle may be placed unlit in the centre of the space. Smaller candles or nightlights may be set next to it, one for each baby to be remembered on that day.

☆ An arrangement of flowers may be placed in the centre of the space.

☆ Individual flower heads may be handed to each person present.

☆ An officiant may be chosen, who may be a member of the family, a friend, or a member of clergy.

Naming prayer

This may be spoken as the decorated name card is placed in the centre of the space.

☆ The mother of the child or the officiant may say a prayer to acknowledge the baby's life using the baby's name, such as:

> At conception N. became an individual person loved by God. When N. died in the womb / shortly after birth / N. began to share in the fullness of life with God.

Psalm

✶ The officiant may read Psalm 139. Alternatively it may be sung (see Chapter 10).

Song

✶ If the psalm is read, the people may sing: 'Be not afraid, I go before you always.'

Bible reading

✶ The officiant may read one or both of the following:
    John 16:33 (You may have peace)
    Romans 8:38–39 (Neither death nor life)

Lighting the candles

✶ The officiant may say 6b – a prayer at lighting the large candle.

✶ The smaller lights may be lit from the large candle, one for each baby to be remembered.

✶ One of the family may say:

    This candle symbolises the life of baby N., now safe in Christ Jesus. When we see the flame burn and feel its warmth we can remember baby N. with our love.

Prayers for the baby

✶ Each person may place a flower in the centre of the room, or a paper with the prayer written on it. Here are some examples of the prayers that might be written:

    Mother:
    Baby N., you were part of me for such a short time but I will never forget you. I have carved your name on my heart.

Father:
With you, O Lord, you have N. whose little heart is joyful within your loving embrace.[3]

Sister/brother:
I never knew you, baby N., but you will always be my sister/brother. I know that God is looking after you for ever.

Grandparent:
Little baby N., we were looking forward so much to welcoming you into our family. I know you are safe now, in God's eternal care.

☆ Those who feel unable to make a prayer can simply place a flower in the centre to say 'I love you, baby N.'

A time of silence follows

Song

☆ The people may sing a song based on Matthew 19:13–15: 'Let the children come to me.'

Prayers for the living

The people present may like to compose their own prayers in readiness for this moment, for the various members of the family and anyone else touched by the death of the baby.

☆ Any member of the group may say one or more of the following:
    3a – a mother's prayer after miscarriage.
    3f – a father's prayer.
    3g – a grandmother's prayer.

Peace

☆ The officiant may say 9a – a prayer for peace.

Final prayer

✩ The officiant may say:

> God our Father, pour out upon us the power of your
> healing love.
> Heal our hearts; renew our spirits.
> Enkindle in us the fire of your love.
> In the life of your Spirit we shall be created,
> And you shall renew the face of the earth.[4]

———

MULTIDENOMINATIONAL SERVICE FOR 10 TO 40 PEOPLE IN A ROOM

It often happens that the first attempt at a baby memorial
service is on a small scale. This was my own experience
when I called a group of twenty-five together in 1993 to
discuss and create a special liturgy for remembering babies
who had died in pregnancy. The liturgy was created in the
space of about an hour, with very few materials to work on
and a feeling of being rushed. However, as an experience
it was very potent and healing. There was an atmosphere
of love, joy, and sorrow all at once, and great feeling of
sharing in something new and precious.

It is my belief that, however uncertain one may be of the
value of such a liturgy, a small-scale experiment can serve
to build confidence in creating a larger event to serve a
greater number of parents.

The following is a compilation of ideas from experimen-
tal liturgies created during two prayer days, one in 1993
and one about a year later. An Anglican priest who was
present in 1994 took up the idea and created a service in
her own parish church that has now become a bi-annual
event.

Choosing the officiant

This service may involve members of clergy of different Christian denominations. It is to be hoped that the various clergy tasks in the liturgy will be shared equally, but experience shows that the service works better if one member of clergy acts as officiant. The service is specially for the parents and they will have a chance to take a real part in what happens, but the whole thing will go more smoothly with someone in charge to provide explanations and instructions about the ritual as it proceeds.

Arranging the room

Chairs are arranged in a circle with exactly the right number of chairs. A double circle is best if the room is small. On the floor, or on a small table, a centrepiece can be created, with a small statue or a simple vase of pansies or bud roses. A large candle is placed near the centrepiece, unlit.

Prayer making

This is an important element of this liturgy, as it enables the full participation of each person. Parents are encouraged each to bring one small item in remembrance of the pregnancy and their baby. This could be the hospital wrist band, an appointment card, any kind of certificate, etc. They will keep these with them until the appropriate moment in the liturgy.

Everyone present is encouraged to write a prayer there and then with reference to a particular baby who has died. Some people may have already chosen a prayer from some printed source. The written prayers can become a treasured memento of the day, and may be used in private prayer in the future, or used in future liturgies.

MODEL LITURGY[5]

✰ Some instrumental music may be played as people gather, and compose their prayers.

✫ The following items may be made available to each member of the congregation:
 A nightlight for each baby to be remembered.
 A sticky label for each nightlight.
 A cut flower on a short stalk.

A period of silence is kept

Introductory remarks

✫ The officiant may say a few words of introduction:

> We have come here as an act of faith, hope and love, in spite of loss, grief, anger and despair. We come to accept the reality of living, to reflect on the miracle of birth and the mystery of death. We have known pain and anguish and we seek the renewal of our will to love.
>
> We have come to be with each other. In the midst of life we have been confronted by the reality of death. We feel a new poignancy, that life is precious. Our children were gone before we knew it. We remember them and we leave them in the hands of God, who is God of the living and not the dead. We are not without hope, and we pray that our faith, strength and courage will be renewed.

Candle

✫ The large candle may be lit by another member of the clergy.

✫ The officiant may say 1d – a prayer to remind everyone of the presence of Christ among them.

Hymn

'Lord of all hopefulness'

Bible readings

☆ The officiant may read one of the following passages:
   Psalm 13 (how long, Lord?)
   Psalm 84:1–5 (a sparrow has found a nest)
   Isaiah 65:17–18 (a new heaven and a new earth)

Prayer over baby items

☆ Parents are invited to come forward and place their baby item near the centrepiece.

☆ As they do this, the officiant may say:

O God in whom is heaven, in our grief we draw strength from each others' presence. May these tokens of our babies reflect our love for them and your love for us all; today and every day.

Naming

☆ The idea of naming may be introduced by another clergy member, for those who have not already given a name to their baby.

Psalm

This may be sung while some people are meditating on the name for their baby.
   Psalm 139 (sung) 'From my beginning' (see page 128)

☆ For each baby to be remembered, one of the parents writes the chosen name on a sticky label and sticks this onto the side of their nightlight.

Readings

☆ One or more parent may read
   R20 – 'The Prophet'
   R32 – 'To Daffodils'
   A piece by one of the parents present

Placing the nightlights

☆ The officiant may explain the procedure as follows:

> A member of each family may come forward with a nightlight, light it from the main candle and place it near the centre, so that the lights form a circle. Some of you may wish to come hand in hand in placing the candle.

☆ While this is done, some music may be played, or a Taizé song such as 'Ubi Caritas'.

The family prayers

☆ The officiant may introduce these prayers in the following way:

> We are now going to circle these babies around with our prayers of thanksgiving, joy and pain. If you would like to read your prayer and place your flower on the table please do. Otherwise just place your flower there silently. Some of you may speak their prayer aloud, some may read it. Some of you may simply bring the folded paper on which is written your prayer.

☆ A parent may say:

> I want to thank you, Lord, for the life of my baby, however short it may have been, for I know that in your eyes his life is just as valuable as any other baby. It was a bittersweet privilege to have been his mother, and now I dedicate him to your care.

☆ A couple may say:

> Thank you, Lord, that you are with us in our pain and loss, and that with your love you will help us to use this experience to grow closer to you.

Hymn

'Make me a channel of your peace'

The Lord's Prayer

✫ The people all join hands in a circle while saying the Lord's prayer together, to emphasise the shared experience of loss.

Final prayer

✫ Another clergy member may say 16b – a prayer summing up the service.

Final blessing

✫ The officiant may say 17e – a blessing.

A period of comforting one another can be appropriate here, depending on the size of the group. Reflective music may be played at this time. It may be helpful after the service if refreshments are served close by to allow people to have time to recover.

———

For I am certain of this: that neither death nor life, no angel, no prince, nothing that exists, nothing still to come, not any power, or height or depth, nor any created thing, can ever come between us and the love of God made visible in Christ Jesus our Lord.
ROMANS 8:38–39 (JB)

6

Baby Memorial Services for Churches and Cathedrals

> *Up, cry out in the night-time*
> *in the early hours of darkness;*
> *pour your heart out like water*
> *before Yahweh.*
> *Stretch out your hands to him*
> *for the lives of your children.*
> LAMENTATIONS 2:19 (JB)

======

ANNUAL BABY MEMORIAL SERVICE FOR A PARISH CHURCH

It is my hope that one day in every Christian parish church the tradition will be created of holding an annual baby memorial service, to enable those parishioners whose babies died during pregnancy to gather as a group and acknowledge the loss of their babies publicly and among friends.

The service is best structured bearing in mind the fact that each parent will have a variety of strong feelings about what happened. Some kind of emotional release will be of benefit. Also an active ritual with the use of symbols will focus grieving and allow the parents to express their love for their babies.

The loss of a baby in pregnancy cuts at the very root of

self-confidence, and often undermines faith in God to the extent that the parents may cease to attend church. A well-advertised special service like this may be the way back for them. Special prayers are needed to strengthen faith in those who have lost trust in God.

Most people attending will be feeling a deep sense of loss, mixed with a paradoxical creative energy that may still remain from a pregnancy cut short. This creativity may find expression in being involved with the service planning or on the day. (See 'Creative parents', p. 120.) Others may not know what they feel, until their tears take them by surprise.

A woman wrote to me some years ago, telling me how after four miscarriages she needed badly to grieve, but her husband refused to acknowledge the loss and would not talk about it. She attended four baby memorial services like this one over almost two years. Gradually, she let her babies go and resigned herself to a possibly childless future. A year later she was delivered of a healthy baby.

The hormones of pregnancy are finely tuned: who is to tell if the stress engendered by the unresolved grief for each miscarried baby was affecting each next pregnancy?[1] Who knows if those four services relieved the woman at last of the burden of grief, and set her free to nurture her next pregnancy to full term?

At least it is clear that in letting go and accepting God's will this mother found peace. The service is designed to facilitate that process for every bereaved parent. It is my hope that, to meet this need, such services will one day be made available throughout the Christian world.

Publicity

Many young parents experience pregnancy loss when they are not settled in one place, but likely to move house at any time. This effect, plus the fact that they may have lost the church-going habit, may mean that they are not in touch with a local church. Baby memorial services should therefore be advertised extensively in the secular press, doctors' surgeries, hospitals, on local radio, etc.

It may be worth making clear that this service is for those who have experienced stillbirth, ectopic pregnancy, and miscarriage. The prayers may not be appropriate for those whose babies died after birth or whose babies were aborted.[2]

Evangelism

Many of those who come to the service may, like many of those who attend funerals in church, be unfamiliar with church services, but if this experience is a satisfying one for them they may return for the next service, or may reappear at Christmas. This is how these services create a chance for parishes to reach out with love and care to those who may not currently be in touch with the church, and bring them in.[3]

Before the service begins

Nightlights with different coloured holders (pink for girls, blue for boys, yellow if not sure) are made available to parents, one for each child. A sticky label with the child's name is placed around the candle. The candles are kept unlit by the parents until an appropriate point in the service. If more than two babies are being remembered, a small tray will be needed to facilitate this.

Individual flower heads are laid in a basket, for any children, fathers and grandparents to take at the appropriate moment in the service.

Cards with the name of the child, date of death and any message are inscribed and placed on a tray.

A visitors' book can be provided in which people can leave names and addresses, so that they may receive an invitation to the next service.

MODEL LITURGY

Entry procession

☆ The officiant may enter, preceded by two people carrying baskets, one of flowers and one of cards.

Opening hymn

'We cannot measure'

☆ The baskets are laid by the altar.

Welcome

☆ The officiant may read a Bible sentence such as Wisdom
4:8, and say 1c – a welcoming prayer.

Bible reading

☆ One or more of the following may be read:
Matthew 18:1–5, 10–14 (become like little children)
2 Corinthians 1:3–7 (comfort us in our sorrow)

Psalm

☆ The choir or congregation may sing Psalm 139 (see page
128).

Penitence

It is important for parents to remember where they may
have failed in faith when their baby died.

☆ The officiant and the people may say 5a – a responsorial
prayer.

Readings

☆ Various passages of poetry or prose may be read:
R14 – 'Footprints'
R22 – 'Joy and sorrow'
R33 – 'A lily of a day'

Lighting candles

☆ The main candle may be lit, and the smaller nightlights lighted from it.

☆ The officiant may say 6a – a prayer on lighting of candles.

Placing the candles

☆ Families may leave their seats and form a procession in the centre aisle, carrying the lighted nightlights.

☆ The basket of flowers may be placed in an accessible spot.

☆ Other family members may take a flower from the basket, one for each baby to be remembered.

☆ The lights may be arranged along with the flowers in front of the altar.

Music

☆ A choir may sing the 'Pie Jesu' from Fauré's Requiem.

or:

☆ The congregation may sing the Taizé chant 'Ubi caritas'.

Name call

☆ For an introduction, the officiant may read Isaiah 43:1 (you are mine).

☆ The names on the cards may be read out by the officiant.

Remembering the babies

☆ A parent may read a prayer of his/her own, such as:

God our Father, who created darkness and light, sorrow and joy, teach us to understand that death is only a part of life. Keep us faithful and hopeful that our babies are safe in your eternal care.

Committal

☆ The officiant may say 11a – a prayer committing the babies to the eternal care of God.

General prayers

☆ One or more of the following may be read:
    12h – a prayer for families.
    4b – a prayer for doctors and nurses.
    12j – a prayer for the childless.

Final prayer

☆ The parents may say prayer 16b together.

Blessing

☆ The officiant may say 17d – a blessing.

Final hymn

'Fleetingly known' (see page 130).

After the service

It is strongly advised that some kind of collection be made as people leave, as this service is expensive to mount. It would be a pity if such services were not provided purely on the grounds of expense. If there is any profit once expenses are covered, this can be donated to an appropriate organisation (see Chapter 14).

The people may appreciate some kind of refreshment, and counsellors can be made available to parents who may be particularly distressed by the service.

The named cards can be sorted into alphabetical order to be returned to the parents if they wish it, and they may also come and claim their nightlights. If they are left behind they may be extinguished and lit again at Christmas.

Any name cards left behind can be displayed on a special board inviting prayers.

=====

A BABY MEMORIAL SERVICE
FOR A CATHEDRAL

In the last ten years parents have felt more able to demand the right to mourn their children openly. No longer is prayer after pregnancy loss and stillbirth a simple private matter. In cathedrals all over the Christian world many hundreds of mourning parents have gathered for special liturgies to remember their babies, sometimes many decades after they died, and often for the very first time.[4]

To attend such a service is to be confronted by tragedy on a grand scale. I attended a service at Guildford Cathedral in 1994. The atmosphere was full of emotion, and the sight of several coaches parked outside gave some indication of the dearth of such services at that time.

The political implications of such a service lie in the example given to other, smaller churches. When I want to impress others with the urgency of this matter, I tell them that there have been services that filled a cathedral, and then the difficulties of mounting a service at parish level seem slight by comparison. A cathedral service is likely to attract a large number of people. A very high degree of planning is required as well as the full cooperation of the dean and precentor.[5]

Organisation

A local group of parents may get together initially and hand out jobs. There are three basic areas to consider: the advance publicity, practical arrangements for the day, and the liturgy.

Publicity

The first step is to decide who will be invited. Will this be just for parents who have suffered stillbirth or pregnancy loss, and if so, will it include abortion? What about neonatal death, cot death, death in infancy or death in childhood? It is so hard to discriminate that ideally all those families in the diocese touched by the death of a child should be invited.

Simply booking a date in the cathedral may need many months' notice. If the idea is for whole families with young children to come, then particularly active toddlers and young children can be entertained in a crèche. This needs to be arranged well in advance. The time of day is important: if the diocese is very large and people may take a long time travelling, then it must not be too early or late in the day, and there should be refreshments afterwards.

Once the date and time are known, the publicity may begin, and as soon as possible. No stone should be left unturned: local radio and television interviews need to be booked well in advance. National organisations (see page 180) may have quarterly or annual newsletters that need copy well in advance. Some women's magazines have been known to give some space to a forthcoming service; it is worth a try, particularly those for parents, or with a religious slant.

A poster can be made, and distributed widely within the diocese. A telephone contact must be chosen (preferably two or three different numbers, to lessen the load). Local papers, hospitals, local organisations, churches and health centres can be contacted a little nearer the time.

Practical arrangements

It is important to have someone knowledgeable answering the telephone, and someone who understands. It may be the first time that the caller has spoken to anyone of the death of her baby since it happened, and she may need time to talk.

A remembrance book can be of help to those who would like to attend but cannot. Also some small cards can be printed in advance for recording the name of each baby to be remembered, and these can be filled in on behalf of those who cannot attend. They may be returned by post after the service, and if a stamped addressed envelope is requested this will reduce the expense.

A collection can be taken for an appropriate organisation, out of which expenses can be deducted. There will be a need for at least ten helpers on the day, and someone to coordinate the whole thing.

Liturgy

An important consideration is the length of the service. If it is too long, young children will become bored; about 25–40 minutes seems right. If the service is to include all parents who have lost a child, then the prayers will have to be fairly broad in scope. A general review of cathedral services reveals three themes: the tragedy of the loss, the fact that the babies are safe in the hands of God and the present needs of the parents for healing and peace of mind.[6]

The desire to create a liturgy for themselves must not lead parents to overburden the liturgy with secular material. A good balance of prayer, Bible readings, hymns, published material and parents' own material may be hard to find, but ultimately everyone must keep in mind that this is a service of prayer.

Using the building

A large cathedral can create a sense of isolation for people standing at the side or at the back. A procession that encircles some parts of the cathedral can help more people to feel included. If some prayers are spoken at the baptistry this will help to diffuse the prayerful atmosphere throughout the building. These days, amplification techniques allow everyone to hear what is being said, wherever they may be in the building, even if they cannot see. If a side chapel or some other site in the cathedral has been dedicated to children, this should be included in some way in the liturgy.

Involving the people

On the whole, bereaved parents share a frustrated desire to do something on behalf of their child. Active involvement is therefore of vital importance if the service is to meet their needs, yet the sheer logistics of allowing a thousand people to participate in enacting a rite may seem too complex. There are ways of overcoming this; for example, if a delegate from every family were to come forward the numbers may be more manageable. Hundreds of candles lit at once are likely to contravene cathedral regulations and create a fire risk. Equally, hundreds of flowers are likely to be very expensive to provide and manage. Name cards are the most sensible and manageable way to make the babies manifest.

Using name cards

For each baby, a specially decorated name card may be purchased before the service and filled in with the name and surname clearly written. This, plus a circular, coloured sticker (blue for a boy, pink for a girl and yellow if not sure) with the baby's name on it, can be handed to a deacon with a microphone who will take the card and read the name.

If the family delegates form a procession to come forward, there need be no gaps in the service: the names can be read out as if a continuous list, at the rate of at least 25 per minute. The cards can be placed in a tray for presentation at the altar and eventual return; the sticker may be given to a lay worker who will stick them onto a tree or vine design (see p. 120) for longer-term display.

Music

Most cathedrals have a choir and this opens the way to more dramatic settings of sacred music. Canticles, anthems and settings of the Psalms can be included in the liturgy to enable the congregation to listen and contemplate, or to accompany procession or ritual.

When there are many hundreds of people gathered together, silence can never be total, and so may lose its effectiveness as an aid to prayer. At times when no words are being spoken or sung, quiet organ or instrumental music may be more effective than total silence. Hymns with well-known tunes, sung by everyone in unison, can display a unity of purpose of all present and guarantee maximum involvement.

Themes

Liturgical themes may vary according to the wishes of the organising team. For example, the liturgy may reflect the grieving process, beginning with shock and despair and moving towards acceptance and peace (see page 115).

Alternatively, the liturgical theme may reflect all the stages of pregnancy from conception to birth, or perhaps the different people touched by the death of a child, starting with the parents and radiating out to include the rest of the family and the workers involved. It may be that the service is intended for parents of any child or baby of any age. If this is so, then it may be helpful to begin with the death of a child and move the focus backwards towards an early miscarriage. (The liturgy below reflects this theme.)

MODEL LITURGY

Entrance

✫ The clergy and readers may process through the building.

Hymn

'There's a friend for little children.'

Welcome

To remind the people of why they are there: to remember their child in sorrow and in love; to support each other in the knowledge of the love of God for all he has made.

✫ The officiant may say:

Grace and peace from the Lord be with you.

All: And also with you.

☆ The officiant may offer 1c – a prayer of welcome.

Readings (The death of a child)

☆ Lay readers may read one or more of the following:
    Mark 10:13–16 (let the children come)
    1 Corinthians 13:4–13 (on love)
    R6 – 'Via dolorosa'
    R8 – 'To a little child born dead'

Prayers of grieving

☆ One of the following may be said:
    2b – a prayer of sorrow.
    2c – a responsorial prayer for mourners.

Procession

☆ The parents (one from each family) are invited to form a procession towards the altar carrying named cards and stickers.

Name call

☆ The names are called out by a deacon, the cards placed on a tray and the stickers mounted on a display.

☆ The tray of cards is carried around the cathedral during the next hymn and finally brought to the altar.

Hymn

'Fleetingly known' (see page 130).

Blessing of cards

☆ The officiant may say prayer 6d – blessing the cards.

Readings (A stillbirth)

☆ Lay readers may read one or more of the following:

98 / *Not Out of Mind*

R9 – 'Still born'
R11 – 'A letter to my baby'
R14 – 'Footprints'

Intercessions

These prayers may be said by chaplains from the various hospitals in the area.

12d – for mothers.
12h – for parents after the death of a baby.
12f – for parents after pregnancy loss.
12j – for all parents.

Psalm 139

✫ This may be read from the Bible, spoken aloud with or without responses, or sung (see page 128).

The committal

✫ The officiant may say 11f – a prayer committing the babies into the care of God.

The Lord's Prayer

✫ This prayer may be said by all the congregation.

Hymn

'Make me a channel of your peace.'

Procession to baptistry (during the hymn)

✫ The tray of names may be taken to the baptistry where it is laid near the font.

✫ Representatives of local organisations helping grieving parents may join the procession and each bring a posy of flowers to place around the tray.

Final remarks

✫ Some informal words from a high-ranking member of clergy are appropriate here, to recognise the work that has gone into the day, the long distances travelled, the burden of grief brought to the service, and the hope that the burden will seem a little lighter when people go home.

Final prayer

✩ The officiant may say 16b – a final prayer.

Blessing

✩ The officiant may say 17a – a solemn blessing.

Retiring hymn

'Lord of all hopefulness'

The tray of cards may be taken from the baptistry and the cards sorted into alphabetical order for parents to collect.

If there are books of remembrance they may be on display. The children's chapel may be reserved for private prayer. Organisers may have to be ready for the unexpected: after the Guildford service in 1994, a couple who mistook the time of the service arrived as it was ending and were in distress, so they were taken to a side chapel where the readings and prayers were re-enacted.

> The chaplain of our local SANDS group and I were able to hold the whole service over again in the children's chapel for this couple and one other lady who had missed the beginning. Having done it for a thousand people I found a strange peace in doing it again for three. It brought home to me the inestimable value of this kind of service, on whatever scale it is organised.[7]

═══

Above the heavens is your majesty chanted
by the mouths of children, babes in arms.

PSALM 8:1b–2 (JB)

7

Special Eucharists

Forgive us our debts,
as we also have forgiven our debtors.
And lead us not into temptation,
but deliver us from the evil one.

MATTHEW 6:12–13 (NIV)

This chapter is intended to show how a celebration of the Eucharist can be helpful when a baby dies as a result of stillbirth, miscarriage or abortion. Two liturgies are described:

☆ A Eucharist healing the pain of the unmourned and unburied.

☆ A Roman Catholic Mass for parents bereaved by the death of a baby.

===

A HEALING EUCHARIST

The callous way that the bodies of stillborn and miscarried babies were once literally thrown away has left its mark in the hearts of many thousands of men and women. They carry scars that may take many years to surface, and may have yet to surface in the next generation. There may be several past members of a family who were not given a proper burial because it was not the custom at the time to do this, but the feelings remain, and demand expression.

Carrying a burden of guilt or grief can become an obsession as unconscious feelings surface inappropriately. These hidden feelings may be translated into inexplicable mental or physical disturbances. It is as though the person is 'possessed' by the spirit of the unburied and unmourned.

To end this sense of 'possession' it is necessary to be 'set free' of the feelings by expressing them at last, making peace with the dead and letting them go. There is therefore a need in the range of liturgies relating to pregnancy loss for a celebration of the Eucharist, which allows a full confession for one's own sins and the sins of others, and which provides a vehicle to hand the dead over to God.

The Lord's Prayer asks that we be delivered from evil, and this can be said during a eucharistic service. Prayers of penitence and asking for forgiveness of others may be hard to make openly, but it is through giving these prayers, sincere and heartfelt, that healing may be obtained. At the offertory, the lives of the unborn and unburied may be given up to God, perhaps symbolised by a family tree marking all members of the family who remain unburied and unmourned.

The Eucharist may be said in the presence of the person who is suffering the symptoms of possession, or may be celebrated on their behalf. Those who come to pray may not themselves be in need of a special Eucharist, but we are all sinners and all in need of prayer, so there is not one person who will not find some benefit.[1]

The following is a compilation of ideas derived from several similar liturgies.

Preparatory prayers for forgiveness
These prayers should be spoken aloud and shared with others we trust – especially family members. It is best in a private Eucharist and prayed before the confessions. If this is included in a public service, then sit outside in the car beforehand. If in a service specially established for this

purpose for many families, then they can come up to the altar during the offertory and lay their family trees and requests there and say aloud their prayers with several families talking at once. Be specific in naming the sins. To say them aloud makes the whole thing objective and takes the symptoms outside the patient.[2]

MODEL LITURGY

Note: There is no music or singing in this liturgy; this is to enable some periods of meditation in a healing silence. To preserve this silence it is suggested that young children not be included, but left in a crèche nearby.

* The people gather in silence.

* Cards may be prepared by each family with the names of those who are to be prayed over.

* Some families may have with them a family tree with the unmourned and unburied clearly marked. They will bring this to the altar during the offertory procession.

Opening Bible verse

* The officiant may read the following verses:
    1 Thessalonians 4:14 (those who have fallen asleep)
    Revelation 7:17 (wipe away all tears)

Opening prayer

* The officiant may offer a prayer to set the tone of this special Eucharist. The emphasis is on confession of sins, the release of those in bondage and healing for those in the family tree who are unburied and unmourned.

> *I am the resurrection and the life. He who believes in me will live, even though he dies; and whoever lives and believes in me will never die.* JOHN 11:25–26a (NIV)

Let us pray:

God our Father in heaven, we bow in your presence

and thank you for sparing your only Son. We know that you, our Lord Jesus Christ, are risen from the dead. You are alive and here with us. Please now direct your angels to gather all our deceased that seem to be lost, especially N. and many others whom you know but whom we have omitted. Bring them where you wish that they may see your broken body, healed and risen so that in their brokenness they might rise.

Let them receive your blood poured out a completed act for the forgiveness of sins. Blind and banish Satan and his minions to their appropriate place. Let the body and blood of our Lord heal all the wounds and torments inflicted by Satan and his minions on the living and dead. Father, we come as stumbling children who neither understand nor know how to pray. Send your Holy Spirit to intercede for us. We ask this in the name of our Lord Jesus Christ. Amen.

The rite of forgiveness

☆ The officiant may say:

We and our departed ones have sinned before you.
Lord, have mercy.
We and our departed ones have failed to forgive one another.
Lord, have mercy.
We and our departed ones have failed to forgive our ancestors.
Lord have mercy.

Confession

☆ The people may say aloud a prayer of confession.

Absolution and deliverance

☆ The officiant may say prayers of absolution followed by prayers of deliverance.

✫ Holy water may be used for cleansing.

Readings

✫ A lay person may read one or more of the following:
    2 Maccabees 12:38–45 (it is good to pray for the dead)
    Isaiah 25:6–9 (wipe away every tear)
    Romans 6:3–9 (if we die with Christ we will live with him)
    1 Corinthians 15:51–57 (death is swallowed up in victory)

Gospel reading

✫ The officiant may read one of the following:
    Luke 18:15–17 (Jesus and babies)
    John 14:1–6 (many mansions)
    1 John 3:1–2 (we shall be like God)

Prayers

✫ One or more of the following prayers may be said:
    10d – for unmourned or unburied aborted babies.
    14a – for unmourned or unburied miscarried babies.
    10a – for unmourned or unburied stillborn babies.

Final prayer

✫ The officiant may say a final prayer:

    O Lord, grant rest to the souls of these babies, that
    they may repose in a place where there is no pain, no
    grief, no sighing but everlasting life. Amen.

Silence

✫ A period of silent prayer may follow.

Offertory

✫ Two plates may be handed round and cards with the names of those who are to be remembered are placed on them. When all the cards are collected the procession starts.

☆ The bread and wine are brought in silence to the altar by two lay people.

☆ Family trees are brought individually by those who have prepared them, and laid around the altar.

☆ To signify the way that the pain of the unburied and unmourned passes through the generations, one plate of cards is brought by an older person or grandparent, the other by a young person or child.

Name call

☆ Before reading out the names, the officiant may say:

Lord God, our Redeemer and Saviour, grant eternal rest to N., N., etc.

☆ The officiant then reads out all the names from the cards.

Eucharistic prayer
(as for a funeral with communion)

Holy, Holy

Prayer of consecration

The Lord's Prayer

☆ The congregation may say this together, and families may join hands, showing their joint wish for deliverance in their family.

Lamb of God

☆ Communion is now received.

106 / *Not Out of Mind*

Prayer after communion

✫ The officiant may say:

> We give you thanks, our God and King, for the joy of
> this heavenly banquet and we beseech you that the
> sacrament of your body and blood may not turn to
> our condemnation but be for us and all the departed,
> especially those we have named in this service, the
> cleansing of sin, the strengthening of weakness and
> our strong defence against all adversity; through
> your mercy, O Saviour of the world, who lives and
> reigns with the Father in the unity of the Holy Spirit,
> one God, world without end.[3]

Anointing

Anointing with oils seals the healing of this service.

Blessing

> May God the Father Almighty continue to heal you
> that you may have more of his love for the living and
> the dead. We ask this blessing in the name of the
> Father and of the Son and of the Holy Ghost. Amen.

Note: Following a Eucharist in the home, or when return-
ing home afterwards, it may be found helpful if a member
of clergy pronounces a blessing upon the house and
sprinkles the doorstep with holy water.

The use of the Lord's Prayer in the matter of deliverance rewards some extra thought. The prayer is rich in
meaning and can be meditated upon for some time. We
can achieve increased awareness of the choice we all have,
to live in bondage or in the power of the Holy Spirit.

A ROMAN CATHOLIC MASS

The Roman Catholic Church has led the field for some years in creating suitable liturgies for the funerals of stillborn and miscarried babies. However, until about ten years ago, for a priest to celebrate Mass for those experiencing pregnancy loss was very unusual. In some parishes this was not for want of trying: some enlightened priests did attempt to hold a regular Mass for those who had suffered a miscarriage, but the practice died out because of a lack of numbers attending, which seemed to indicate that this kind of service was not needed.[4]

Today, as the whole issue of pregnancy loss is receiving so much publicity, there is more demand. Hospital-based memorial services are usually multidenominational, and this can leave Roman Catholic parents feeling that they have not expressed their grief within the Mass, in the normal parish setting.

A Requiem Mass is not really suitable for this kind of service, for as we saw in the last chapter, there is a need to say both a 'hello' and a 'goodbye'. However, there is place for some of the prayers from the funeral of a stillborn or miscarried child.

The liturgy given below was published in 1987, and was one of the first of its kind.[5] A woman who had suffered four miscarriages, and was childless as a result, began to realise some years later that she needed a liturgy. A small group of women in Newcastle got together and planned it. They were all of the same mind: that there was no public affirmation of their children's lives, no chance to set aside private sorrow, no ritual gestures that would enact a surrender of their babies to God. Understandably, there was a certain amount of bitterness at the time that Roman Catholic clergy, who have always stood so firmly by the belief that life begins at conception, should delay in meeting the needs of those whose babies died in pregnancy with a Mass just for them.[6] Happily, in the subsequent ten years, the situation has changed. It is now much more common, in Roman Catholic churches up and down the country, to celebrate a regular Mass 'For all God's little ones'.[7] The liturgy given below is a model of what can be done.

MODEL LITURGY

'Celebrating brief lives': a mass for babies who die during pregnancy

☆ Small candles may be made available for each person present.

Opening hymn

☆ All the people may sing 'Fleetingly known'.

Welcoming remarks

☆ The officiant may welcome those who may not be regular attenders, as well as members of the usual congregation.

> We welcome today those among you who are parents bereaved by the loss of a baby in pregnancy. This is a special, hidden and often secret loss, but today at last we can bring all those feelings into the open and share them. We welcome the children, whose sisters and brothers they never knew; we welcome grandparents who have suffered the loss of a grandchild.

> We remember today all those who cannot be here, and all those who have no prayer to offer because their grief has overcome their faith. We hope and pray that the day will come when their faith is renewed, and they too will feel ready to join us in another special Mass in this place.

Penitential rite

☆ The congregation may say the following prayer together:

For the times when we have not turned to you in our need
Lord, have mercy.
For the times when we have blamed ourselves or others unjustly
Christ, have mercy.
For the smallness of our faith
Lord, have mercy.
Let us pray:
Merciful God, hear our prayer and console us as we renew our faith in your Son whom you raised from the dead. Strengthen our hope that our departed children will share in his resurrection. Through Christ our Lord. Amen.

Bible reading

☆ A lay person may read one or both of the following:
Psalm 139:13–16 (you created my inmost self)
Isaiah 65:17–20 (new heavens and new earth)

Gospel acclamation

☆ The people may say together:

Alleluia, Alleluia. The will of my Father, says the Lord, is that I should lose nothing of all that he has given to me, and that I should raise it up on the last day. Alleluia.

Gospel

☆ The officiant may read the following:
Matthew 18:1–4 (little children)

Renewal of baptismal vows

The officiant may say:

> We express our belief in the life of our children with Christ. Standing together with them in the presence of God and in the communion of saints we repeat our baptismal vows.

☆ The renewal of vows follows the form of the Easter Vigil service.

Bidding prayers

☆ The officiant may introduce the prayers:

> Let us turn to God with our prayers that the spirit of forgiveness and healing may be in us.

☆ A reader may offer these prayers, or others, specially created for the occasion:

> We pray for the departed children of all here present. We hand them into the arms of God. Lord, hear us.
> *Lord, graciously hear us.*
> We pray for all aborted children, that they may know the eternal love of their creator. Lord, hear us.
> *Lord, graciously hear us.*
> We pray for the parents of aborted children, that they may recognise and accept the loving forgiveness of God. Lord, hear us.
> *Lord, graciously hear us.*
> We pray for those who wrongly blame themselves for the loss of a child, that they may find forgiveness and healing. Lord, hear us.
> *Lord, graciously hear us.*
> We pray for all those who have hurt and angered us in our grief by not comprehending our loss. Lord, hear us.
> *Lord, graciously hear us.*

☆ The officiant may sum up as follows:

Father, we give thanks for your imponderable ways. Our lives are marked with creative suffering. We offer you our weakness, sorrow and tears, through Christ our Lord. Amen.

Lighting candles

☆ The nightlights are lit from the Paschal candle, a server with a taper passing down the aisle.

☆ The officiant may say 6a – a prayer at the lighting of candles.

Offertory procession

☆ The bread and wine is brought by a couple whose baby died.

☆ The nightlights, still burning, are brought by a member of each family and laid together in front of the altar.

Offertory hymn

☆ A hymn is sung during the procession: 'All that I am'.

Eucharistic prayer

☆ The prayer for children.

Prayer over the gifts

☆ The officiant may say:

Lord, we are united in this sacrament by the love of Jesus Christ. Accept these gifts and receive your children into the glory of your Son, who is Lord for ever and ever.

Acclamation

Christ has died.
Christ is risen.
Christ will come again.

Prayer after communion

Lord, may this Eucharist we have shared fill us with your courage in the fullness of eternal joy in the communion of saints. We ask this through Christ our Lord.

Blessing

✩ The officiant may say 17a – a solemn blessing.

Final hymn

✩ All the people may sing 'Lord of all hopefulness'.

═══

Come to me, all you who labour and are overburdened, and I will give you rest. MATTHEW 11:28 (JB)

PART TWO

EXTRA RESOURCES

8

Places and Times

There is a time for everything,
and a season for every activity under heaven.
ECCLESIASTES 3:1 (NIV)

This chapter deals with the process of grieving and how this can be facilitated by providing a focus for feelings in two principal ways:

✩ Creating a place dedicated to the memory of a baby.

✩ Deciding on a special time set aside to remember.

When grieving begins
Grieving is seen by some as a process, because there seems to be a way through the darkness into a time when the loss can be integrated into normal daily life, even though sorrow and a deep sense of loss may remain.[1] The first stage is of numbness, when the reality of the death may be denied. After the death of a baby in pregnancy, this denial can last many years.

If a trigger to feelings can be created, at last the reality of the loss can begin to seep through. Those around the bereaved, perhaps disturbed to see that there have been no tears yet, are glad to see the tears begin: 'the grieving process has begun at last'. Once the feelings surface, they can be recognised as anger, depression, loneliness, anxiety and all sorts of other feelings besides. This stage is the most distressing for all to share and endure, but there is love for the baby and a good deal of healing in the tears. To sort out the confusion it is good to talk. The usual tactful response of 'not upsetting' the bereaved is not helpful, for they are not made to cry by talking. The tears are already there but need help in order to fall: the bereaved parent needs support from those who understand this.[2]

Grief has no focus

In the normal event of a death, there is a body to hold and care for in death and to bury with due ceremony; there is a place where the dead can be remembered; there is an anniversary when the memories are more acute and grief can resurface. These focuses are not available in the event of pregnancy loss, and only recently have they been available after stillbirth.

PLACES

Some people die but are not buried in any particular place. Burned in terrible fires, torn apart by explosions, or flushed down the sluice, they are out there somewhere, but yet they are nowhere. In these circumstances the bereaved have a problem with the normal needs of grieving.

A curious but predictable effect is to yearn for the lost beloved and imagine they have come back, or that they are still there in some form. There may be a period of searching, even expressed as literally wandering across the landscape looking for what cannot be found. In the time after birth, some bereaved mothers sleepwalk, imagining they hear their dead baby crying in the night.[3] If the baby died some time ago and it is not known where it is buried, the mother may find herself wanting to know where the baby may be, and writing to the hospital to find out.

Finally, if it can be accepted that the loved one will not be coming back and that life can continue in their absence, then they can be let go to the place where they now must be. Grieving now becomes an enduring sense of loss, intensified occasionally by anniversaries and reminders. When these reminders occur and there is a place to go, then this can help.

Graves and outdoor memorials

Individual memorials

Where a communal grave was used many years ago, the parents may wish to place a small memorial in another more appropriate place. Cemeteries and crematorium gardens are trying to meet this need by setting aside some proportion of their land for baby memorial. There are various ideas that seem to work: large smooth rocks arranged among shrubs, or a long and winding low wall, can act as places to put a small plaque. A garden may be laid out in the form of a flower or clover leaf. A central theme may add to the beauty of the spot. A snowdrop garden is a lovely idea: not only is a portion of the ground laid out in the shape of a snowdrop, but in early spring drifts of white snowdrops, suggesting a host of tiny lost lives, appear out of the grass at a time of year when all seems darkness and cold.[4]

The principal difficulty with providing appropriate memorials is the sheer number of baby deaths: in the UK in 1993, 36% of conceptions were lost – in a year that was unremarkable for pregnancy loss statistics. (This loss includes miscarriages, abortions, ectopic pregnancies and stillbirths.) If each one of these losses were to receive a memorial, then in a few years the sheer scale of pregnancy loss would be quite visible, if not overwhelming. Happily, today all stillborn babies have a grave or memorial plaque and, even if the parents were too stunned or too ill to attend the funeral, later when denial fades there is a place to go, and for parents like this the first visit to this special place may be the trigger to the healing tears of grieving.

Communal memorials

Miscarried babies usually have no grave, even today. The option is offered to parents but not always taken up, and the decision depends on how close to stillbirth the miscarriage came. For miscarriage, the most effective memorial is a communal one. This may be at the local graveyard or crematorium, another piece of public land, or, if a church has a little private land, a small memorial may be erected.

Memorial stone

Inscription: 'Remember all the little ones buried here. Remember also their families who grieve for them.'

Seats

* A bench inscribed with the words: 'In memory of all babies lost to parents in this parish.'

* A stone seat with sculpted figures of baby animals and an inscription: 'In memory of God's little ones.'

Sculpture

* The figure of a sleeping baby, set in a miniature rose garden with the inscription: 'Heaven's gift returned.'

* A small statue of Mary with Jesus as a baby set in a low stone arch with a seat nearby for contemplation and prayer.

Gardens

* Special areas of open land where babies can be remembered while children play and parents sit.

* A flower bulb can be planted in memory of each baby to create a show of flowers in spring and summer.

* A miniature rose bush can be planted for each stillborn baby in small, circular rose gardens. Each plant can have a metal engraved name plaque that can be moved to the side later when the bush dies.

* Brick paths may be created in a pattern across grass, each brick in memory of a child.

In each case, bulbs, plants, bricks, plaques, etc. may be put in place during a group ritual for parents, held periodically at the place where they are to be laid, in an echo of the funeral service.

Indoor memorials

In some churches it is possible to dedicate part of the church to children or babies. For example, Guildford Cathedral in England has a children's chapel. Some churches have alcoves or side chapels that lend themselves to this.[5]

☆ Paintings, usually of Mary, mother of God, in various stages of pregnancy or with Baby Jesus, can provide a backdrop for the smallest side chapel.

☆ Wooden carvings can express various aspects of pregnancy loss. Examples are Mary with a tiny baby held to her heart, with a quotation from the Magnificat. Also, open hands with a sleeping baby resting on them with a quotation from Isaiah. A sculpture of a distraught woman displaying an empty womb to the world may not have any direct religious connotation, but it can make a stark and moving reminder of the grief of pregnancy loss.[6]

☆ Windows may be created using hundreds of tiny pieces of stained glass, each piece dedicated to a particular baby and signed with initials, either before or after glazing.

☆ Tiny mosaic tiles, on the floor, walls or even ceiling of a cloister or aisle, or around the walls of a baptistry, can be dedicated to babies who have died, and glazed after being inscribed with the date. It is suggested that a tile be chosen by the parents for each baby remembered for the first time at a particular service, and placed in a basket made available for the purpose. Each set of tiles can be dated, glazed and mounted by an expert tiler in due course. Different coloured tiles may be handed out for each service so that as years pass a pattern can be created.

☆ A tree may be drawn or painted, or a climbing vine, with each child commemorated with a leaf or grape. This may be done with names handed in at baby memorial services.

☆ Baby memorial books can be created, with names and details taken from cards or special forms filled in by the parents. There may be space for a message or quotation, and the words are written in by a calligrapher. They can be placed where the pages may be viewed by parents who wish to visit. The book may be brought in ceremony to the altar during a memorial service.

☆ Candles may be sold in pink, blue or yellow holders, inscribed with the quotation: 'Let the little children come to me.' The colour may be selected by bereaved parents according to the sex of the baby. The candles may be taken home or lit in the church and left in a special stand to burn in memory of the baby.

Creative parents

☆ A patchwork quilt may be made each year from pieces given by local bereaved parents, each in memory of a child.

☆ Kneelers, each stitched by bereaved parents in memory of their child.

☆ A posy of flowers created and donated by each bereaved parent to decorate the church on a particular day (see below).

☆ A tree covered with labels each with the name of a miscarried baby, displayed at Christmas time.[7]

☆ A temporary mural of Bethlehem made for Christmas with a silver star for each miscarried baby and a gold star for each stillbirth.

TIMES

The anniversary of a baby's death may be known in the case of a stillbirth or abortion, but unclear if the baby died in the womb. To meet this need, a particular day could be set aside for remembering babies lost in pregnancy.

The Feast of the Holy Family (December 29th) is a time to remember all children, living and dead.

The Feast of the Holy Innocents (December 31st) is appropriate for remembering babies lost by abortion, and is already widely used as such.

Candlemas (February 1st) is the Feast of the Presentation of Jesus and may be appropriate.

The Annunciation (March 25th) has associations with conception and pregnancy.

All Souls' Day (October 31st) is traditionally a day to pray for the dead.

The month of November is traditionally a time for Christians to remember their dead.

The Feast day of St Jane Francis of Chantal (December 12th) has been suggested as a day of prayer for mothers who have lost children. St Jane Francis was a sixteenth-century abbess, and buried two children in their infancy.[8]

Whatever day is chosen, it may be marked in several ways: special prayers may be said at public services; special prayer services may be held, stories published in parish newsletters and magazines, collections taken on behalf of local organisations giving support after pregnancy loss, and talks given by representatives of these organisations. The church may be decorated with the creative efforts of bereaved parents and the memorial book may be displayed.

Time for prayer

In many countries it was once traditional to say the

Angelus at various times of the day. A certain time of day could be set aside for a short prayer such as this. Early morning is a good time, suggesting the short time these babies lived. A stillborn baby may be better remembered at bed time, with its associations with parenthood. An example may be:

> Heavenly Father, I will spend this moment with you, remembering N.
> Bless and keep my baby, Lord, until we meet again. Amen.

———

Ask, and it will be given to you; search, and you will find; knock, and the door will be opened to you. MATTHEW 7:7 (JB)

9

Useful Bible References

Search in the book of Yahweh, and read . . . ISAIAH 34:16 (JB)

Note: The references below are as given in the Revised Standard Version of the Bible.

OLD TESTAMENT

2 Kings 20:5   I have seen your tears
Job 11:7–8   The mystery of God
Psalm 13   How much longer?
Psalm 23   The Lord is my shepherd
Psalm 25:4–7, 17, 20   Let me know your ways
Psalm 30:2, 11–12   You have healed me, I praise you
Psalm 40:1–3   He listened to me
Psalm 42:1–3, 11   Why so downcast?
Psalm 61:1–3   Hear my cry
Psalm 63:1–8   I am seeking you
Psalm 84:1–3   The sparrow has found a home
Psalm 91:11   In the angels' charge
Psalm 102:1–2   Let my cry reach you
Psalm 130:1–2   Out of the depths
Psalm 139:13–16   You created my inmost self
Ecclesiastes 3:1–8   A time for dying
Ecclesiastes 11:5   You cannot know the work of God
Isaiah 12:2   My strength my song
Isaiah 25:6–9   Destroy death
Isaiah 40:11   Like a shepherd

Isaiah 43:1–2   You are mine
Isaiah 49:1, 15–16   Forget the baby at the breast?
Isaiah 60:20   Your days of mourning ended
Isaiah 61:1–2   To comfort the mourning
Isaiah 65:17–25   New heavens and new earth
Jeremiah 1:4–5   Before I formed you I knew you
Jeremiah 9:17–18   Call the mourning women!
Lamentations 3:17–26   I have forgotten happiness
Lamentations 3:31–33, 55–57   You heard my cry
Jonah 2:2–7   From the belly of Sheol I cried

NEW TESTAMENT

Gospels

Matthew 5:3–5   The beatitudes
Matthew 10:30   The sparrows fall
Matthew 11:29–30   My yoke is easy
Matthew 18:1–5, 10–14   Become like little children
Mark 10:13–16   Let the children come
Luke 1:29–31   The annunciation
Luke 1:39–45   Mary's pregnancy
Luke 8:4–8   The parable of the sower
Luke 9:46–48   Welcome a child in my name
Luke 18:15–17   Let the little children come
John 6:37–40   I will raise it up at the last day
John 14:1–6   I leave you peace
John 14:27   There are many rooms

Epistles

Romans 6:3–9   New life through baptism
Romans 8:38–39   Neither life nor death
Romans 14:8–9   Alive or dead we belong
1 Corinthians 13:4–13   On love
1 Corinthians 15:51–52   We shall all be changed
2 Corinthians 1:3–7   Comfort in our sorrows
2 Corinthians 5:1   An everlasting home
Ephesians 3:16–19   Paul's blessing: utter fullness of God

Philippians 4:7   The peace of God
1 John 3:1–2   We are God's children
Revelation 7:17   Wipe away all tears
Revelation 21:1–4   A new heaven and earth

PSALM 139

Psalm 139 is particularly useful for services after pregnancy loss. A simplified version is given here:

> You, Lord, created every part of me,
> You put me together in my mother's womb.
> I praise you because you are to be feared;
> All you do is strange and wonderful.
> I know it with all my heart.
> When my bones were being formed,
> Carefully put together in my mother's womb,
> When I was growing in secret,
> You knew that I was there –
> You saw me before I was born.

(A song based on this psalm, with music, can be found on page 128.)

—

Consequently, faith comes from hearing the message, and the message is heard through the word of Christ. ROMANS 10:17 (NIV)

10

Music

Sing to the LORD *a new song,*
his praise from the ends of the earth,
you who go down to the sea, and all that is in it.

ISAIAH 42:10 (NIV)

SUITABLE HYMNS

(Taken from *Hymns Old and New*, Kevin Mayhew 1983)

  4 Abide with me
 31 All things bright and beautiful
 32 All ye who seek a comfort sure
 58 Be still and know that I am God
 59 Be still, my soul
 68 Matthew 5 (Beatitudes)
119 Deep calls to deep
184 Going home
189 Grant us your peace, O Lord
242 Immortal, invisible
254 In you my God may my soul find its peace
282 Jesus heals me
293 Kumbaya
295 Lay your hands gently upon us
297 Lead, kindly light
329 Lord of all hopefulness
337 Love divine, all loves excelling
342 Make us a channel of your peace

431 O the word of my Lord
449 Praise my soul the King of heaven
528 The King of Love my shepherd is

Hymns based on suitable scriptures

Psalm 130: Out of the depths I cry to thee 155, 656, 156
Psalm 139: You knew me in the womb 620, 410, 472
Psalm 23: The Lord is my shepherd 528, 530, 533, 534
Isaiah 43: I have called you by your name 122
Isaiah 43: Do not be afraid, I have redeemed you 627, 122
Isaiah 49: I have carved you in the palm of my hand 265
Jeremiah 1:5: Before I formed you in the womb 431
Matthew 11:28: All who are heavy laden 228, 108, 109
John 6 & 11: I will raise him up on the last day 226, 532
Romans 8: Nothing can ever take us from his love 231
1 Corinthians: Without love my words ring hollow 232

Other suitable hymns

'When our confidence is shaken.' F. Pratt Green
'Have faith in God my heart.' Bryn Rees
'In Heavenly love abiding.' Anna Letitia Waring
'O Lorde the maker.' Anthem by John Joubert
'God is love, let heaven adore him.' Timothy Rees
'Saviour again to thy dear name we raise.' John Ellerton
'Dear Lord and Father of mankind' J. H. Newman
'Loving shepherd of thy sheep.' Jane E. Leeson

OTHER MUSIC

MAHLER: 5th symphony (Adagietto)
ALLEGRI: Miserere
FAURE: Requiem: Pie Jesu
LLOYD WEBBER: Requiem: Pie Jesu
BACH: Jesu, Joy of man's desiring
ALBINONI: Adagio for organ and strings
Taizé chants (various)
Gregorian chants (Ave maria, Miserere)
Guitar music

SONGS AND HYMNS IN FULL

From My Beginning

Words: Althea Hayton (based on Psalm 139)
Music: Mark Underwood

From my beginning you marked all my days.
You know all my thinking, you know all my ways.
Sitting and standing, walking and lying,
Waking and sleeping, laughing and crying.
  I praise you O Lord for this great mystery!
  The wonder of you and the wonder of me!

Even before I was born I was yours,
Set like an arrow upon my life's course.
In the womb's darkness a new life was growing.
You carefully made me, your power all-knowing.
  I praise you . . .

You knew all the intricate secrets of me:
Legs made for dancing and eyes made to see.
A mind made for thinking and knowing your ways,
Ears made to listen, a mouth for your praise.
  I praise you . . .

From my beginning you called me by name:
You are eternal and always the same.
I praise you O Lord for this great mystery!
The wonder of you and the wonder of me!

Fleetingly Known

Words: Anonymous[1]
Tune: Bunessan (commonly known as 'Morning has broken')

Fleetingly known, yet
Ever remembered,
These are our children
Now and always:
These whom we see not
we will forget not,
Morning and evening
All of our days.

Lives that touched our lives,
tenderly, briefly
Now in the one light
living always;
named in our hearts now
safe from all harm now,
We will remember all of our days.

As we recall them,
silently name them,
open our hearts Lord
Now and always:
Grant to us grieving
love for the living:
strength for each other
all of our days.

Safe in your peace Lord
hold these your children;
Grace, light and laughter
grant them each day:
Cherish and hold them
till we may know them
When to your glory
we find a way.

We Cannot Measure

Words: John and Graham Moule[2]
Tune: 'Ye banks and braes'

We cannot measure how you heal
Or answer every sufferer's prayer
Yet we believe your grace responds
Where faith and doubt unite to care.
Your hands though bloodied on the cross
Survive to hold and heal and warn,
To carry all through death to life
And cradle children yet unborn.

The pain that will not go away
The guilt that clings from things long past,
The fear of what the future holds
Are present as if meant to last.
But present too is love which tends
The hurt we never hoped to find,
The private agonies inside,
The memories that haunt the mind.

So some have come who need your help
And some have come to make amends,
As hands which shaped and saved the world
Are present in the touch of friends.
Lord, let your Spirit meet us here
To mend the body mind and soul
To disentangle peace from pain
And make a broken people whole.

11

Further Prayers

And pray in the Spirit on all occasions with all kinds of prayers and requests. EPHESIANS 6:18 (NIV)

1. WELCOME

1a   A memorial service or funeral

May Christ Jesus who welcomed children and laid his hand in blessing upon them, comfort you with his peace and always be with you.
And with you.[1]

1b   A funeral

Lord God, we meet at this moment in sadness and regret. But we thank you for making us aware of the value of life. The pain we feel is a measure of our love for N., our child. Out of the pain of Christ's death for us, make us aware of the love in which you hold us; and over the coming months grant us the strength to bear our loss and the wisdom to know that the life of our child is now in your care, through Jesus Christ our Lord, who through life brought us love and through death gave us hope. Amen.[2]

1c   A memorial service

Lord God, creator of all things, shower your love on the innocent souls of all babies throughout the world, especially those who have died. Comfort these parents in their grief, and grant them your peace.[3]

1d A small group

Gentle Jesus, you promised that if two or three gather in your name you will be there, and that the kingdom of heaven belongs to little children. Be with us now as we pray together.[3]

1e A memorial service

May the peace, compassion and hope that is God be with you in this moment and in the days ahead.
And with you.
We are today in the face of severe loss. We are over-whelmed as we reflect upon the mystery of life and death. We pause silently as we reflect on this mystery, the pain of our grief and our love for baby N. and each other.[4]

1f A funeral

We are gathered here at a very sad time. We were looking forward to a time of joy, and instead there is sorrow. Our feelings of loss and grief are hard to bear. It is hard to understand why baby N. has been taken from us. But there are truths which we can hold on to: God our Creator loves us all, and through his Son Jesus Christ he has promised that he will not leave us or forsake us. Nothing in death nor life can separate us from his love.[5]

1g Any service

We offer our prayer in the name of God, our beginning and end;
In the name of Jesus, God embodied in our humanity;
In the name of the Holy Spirit, sweet dew of heaven.[4]

1h A family service or small group

We have gathered to remember a life/lives growing with N. (these mothers) who has/have not survived the struggle of beginning. We pause in quiet reflection to recall our hopes for this/these child/children who lived in our warmth and remain part of our lives and memory.[4]

1j   A funeral

We come here today to commend baby N. to our heavenly Father, and to commit his/her body to be cremated; to assure you of the everlasting love of God, to share in your sorrow, and to offer you comfort and support.[6]

2. GRIEVING

2a   After a stillbirth

Lord, this dreadful thing has happened, and our minds are baffled, our spirits weighed down with grief.

It is beyond our understanding why this little life should be taken, or why we should be called upon to suffer so terrible a loss.

Yet we know that life is full of mystery and that so many others at this time are facing the same problem and enduring the same anguish as ourselves.

Help us to bear our sorrow without bitterness, and not to question your love; for to whom can we turn for comfort but to you, O Lord?

Speak your word of peace to our hearts; ease our pain and lift our darkness; and be to us a very present help in trouble; for Jesus Christ's sake.[7]

2b   After any loss

Our Father, grant us, this day, the sense of your presence to cheer, and your light to direct us, and give us strength for your service. You know we cannot bear our burdens alone. We are only little children, and the world seems very dark to us, and our path very hard, if we are alone. But we are your little children, so we know we can come to our Father to ask you to help us, enliven us, strengthen us and give us hope. We are not ashamed of our tears, for our Lord has wept with us. We do not ask you to take away our sorrow, for he was made perfect through suffering: but we do ask you to be with us as you were with him, our Father, close to your little ones, even as he has promised us.[8]

2c   After miscarriage or stillbirth

Creator God, when our babies were growing in the womb they were already known to you.
Blessed are those who mourn, for they shall be comforted.
God our Father, before they were born you knew them by name.
Blessed are those who mourn, for they shall be comforted.
Lord of Life, we know our children will never be forgotten. You hold them in the palm of your hand.
Blessed are those who mourn, for they shall be comforted.
Lord Jesus, we know you are with us always, even to the ending of the world.
Blessed are those who mourn, for they shall be comforted.
Spirit of God, sustain us and renew us as we mourn our children.
Blessed are those who mourn, for they shall be comforted.[3]

2d   After any loss

Dear Lord, you seem so far away. In our sorrow we cry to you but we cannot hear you answer. Please do not turn your face from us but bring us through this time to your healing and peace.[3]

2e   After a stillbirth

Mother: You promised comfort to those who mourn. To you we pray:
(All:) Bless us and keep us, O Lord.
Father: We know that neither life nor death can separate us from your love. To you we pray:
Bless us and keep us, O Lord.
Mother: You became a little child for our sake, sharing in our human life. To you we pray:
Blessed are those who mourn, for they shall be comforted.
Father: You welcomed children and promised them your Kingdom. To you we pray:
Blessed are those who mourn, for they shall be comforted.

Officiant: Lord Jesus, whose mother stood grieving at the foot of the cross,
look kindly on these parents who have suffered the loss of their child.
Listen to the prayers of Mary on their behalf,
that their faith may be strong like hers and find its promised reward,
for you live for ever and ever. Amen.[1]

2f   After any loss

I took my burden to the Lord
to cast and leave it there,
I knelt and told him of my plight
and wrestled deep in prayer.
But rising up to go my way
I felt a deep despair,
for as I tried to trudge along
my burden was still there.
Why didn't you take my burden Lord?
Oh won't you take it please?
Again I asked the Lord for help
His answering words were these:
'My child, I want to help you out;
I long to take your load.
I want to bear your burden too
as you walk along life's road.
But this you must remember
This one thing you must know –
I cannot take your burden
until you let it go.[9]

3. THE FAMILY PRAYS

3a   Mother after miscarriage

Loving heavenly Father, I praise you for the new life which you entrusted to me for such a short time. I praise you because you have taken him back to yourself. But

Father, my heart breaks, because I love that child. I wanted to hear his cries, to see his soft features, to hold him, to feel his strong hunger at my breast, to care for him, to watch him grow.

I will always love him. Yet, Father, I know that you love him far more, and so I release him to your care, not understanding but trusting you.

I ask this in the name of our Saviour, Jesus Christ, who cared so deeply for children and their mothers.[10]

3b   Parents after miscarriage

O Lord our God, for a time you gave us the hope of a new life,
Placed in us the expectation of a new awakening.
Now in your wisdom you have taken that hope from us.
The pain of our disappointment is real and deep;
But we acknowledge that you are God;
You renew life beyond death,
You give and you take away
You hold us in the palm of your hands.[11]

3c   A grieving parent's prayer

I feel unable to pray – I need your insight in new ways to pray.
I feel abandoned – I need your warmth.
I feel isolated from you – I need courage to take steps closer to you.
I feel hurt – I need your healing.
I feel so sad – I need your closeness and humour.
I feel anger, resentment and bitterness – I need your peace.
I feel afraid – I need your strength.
I feel anxious – I need your patience.
I feel that I can never trust you again – I need to feel your love.[12]

3d   Parents after stillbirth

It does not make sense, O God.
Why allow us to prepare for a birth

only to receive a death?
Help us to trust in your goodness and wisdom
when our understanding fails.
We ask you this day for courage
and growing discernment
of your loving purposes. Amen.[13]

3e   Mother after abortion

Lord Jesus, please care for my baby. Although my baby
was precious to me, lying deep within me and almost part
of me, I couldn't cope. My baby, I will never forget you,
and in my heart you will continue to grow through the
years, until we meet again.[3]

3f   A father after stillbirth

O God, why did our baby die, why did you let it happen?
We are lost and bewildered and our hearts are full of tears,
because N., the baby we longed for, will never come to be
with us. Please be near us now, holding us as we pray for
knowledge of your ways. We praise you for the mystery of
your love in death and in life. All-knowing, all powerful
God, we place all our trust in you, now and always.[3]

3g   A grandmother after a stillbirth

Dear Lord, you gave us a daughter, a gift from heaven,
many years ago, and let us keep her until she became a
mother. Give me so much love that I can comfort her, so
much strength that I can help her to bear this pain, and so
much faith that we can all keep believing in your infinite
mercy. Amen.[14]

3h   A group of parents

Lord, you stand by us in our grief and anger. Acknowledge our expectancy in love, our hope of birth, our deep
pain on the loss of a little child. You – who know the kin-
ship of flesh, blood and spirit, born of Mary.

Help us to look beyond the loss, the anger and the
anguish to the fulfilment of our children in a kingdom of

your making. You said, 'My kingdom belongs to such as these – let the little ones come to me.' You took them in your arms and blessed them, and you do so still.[2]

3i   A group of parents

God of Hope, we come to you in shock and grief and confusion of heart. Help us to find peace in the knowledge of your loving mercy to all your children, and give us light to guide us out of our darkness into the assurance of your love.[15]

4. WORKERS

4a   A doctor's prayer

'Mary loves you
As you would wish a mother to love a child.'

You have granted me a little enthusiasm, my reward, thank you.
Grant that, for their sake, I may be guided
by sober consideration.

Jesus wept – at Man's folly
Jesus loved – by Mary.
I beg of you that children born and unborn may know such love.
Mary, immaculate conception
Sorrowful for the way Man treats your Son
for the way you are cast as an obstacle on the road to truth.
May I continue to share your burden, as the carpenter.
May my tears be of comfort and support, that the children may know such love.[16]

4b   A prayer for doctors and nurses

Lord Jesus, who healed the sick and gave them new life, be with doctors and nurses as they act as agents of your healing touch. In desperate times keep them strong yet loving and, when their work is done, be with them in their tears as they share with parents the sorrow of losing a child.[3]

5. PENITENCE

5a Any service

Lord God, you know the secrets of every heart.
Lord, have mercy.
Please forgive the hurts we may have given others by our anger.
Christ, have mercy.
Help us to forgive ourselves as we grieve for our babies.
Lord, have mercy.[3]

5b After abortion

Bless us, O Lord, because we all fall short,
our flaws and weaknesses lead us astray;
protect us, Lord.

I nailed my Redemption to a tree
and there he hung and pleaded for me.
Let me rest my head upon thy feet
my woes and hurts your heart to meet.[17]

5c After miscarriage

Lord God, help us to forgive those who have hurt us by not acknowledging our grief. Help them to respect the deep love of every mother for her unborn child, and to see clearly that every tiny new life is a glorious new creation made possible only by you.[3]

6. CANDLES AND CARDS

6a Several small candles

God our Father, source of all light, you revealed Christ to us as the light of the world. May these candles dispel the darkness in our hearts and illuminate us with the brightness of the Holy Spirit. May these tiny lights be a reminder to us that the light of your presence lives in us all, even from the first moments of our existence.[3]

6b   One large candle

This light symbolises the love of Christ in our lives. Jesus said, 'I am the light of the world. Whoever follows me will not walk in darkness but will have the light of eternal life.' Be with us, Lord. Amen.[2]

6c   Candles

Creator God, you sent your Son to die for us, that we may live in the hope of the resurrection. May the light of Christ, who came into the world, be with us in this dark time.[2]

6d   Cards

Lord God, such is your care for all you have made that you mark the fall of every sparrow. Bless these cards that bear the names of beloved babies and children who have died and are now born again in you. May these cards become a treasured memory and reminder of their brief lives.[3]

7. NAMING THE BABIES

7a   Individual parent

God, our loving Father, you have called each one of us by name for all eternity: confident in your embracing love we name our baby N.[2]

7b   A small group

On this candle is the name we were unable to speak before.
Heavenly Father, watch over us as we mourn for N.
May our baby N. live on in our hearts, and in the hearts of everyone here today.[3]

7c   A family

Lord, you formed this child in the womb;
you have known it by name before time began.

142 / *Not Out of Mind*

We now wish to name this little one N.:
a name that we shall treasure in our hearts for ever.[1]

8. SILENCE

8a   After a period of silent contemplation

God gives us silence in our sorrow,
Silent tears to speak our grief.
Come into our silence, Lord,
Where in the holiness of your love
There is no need for words.[3]

9. PRAYERS FOR PEACE

9a   Any service

May Christ give to you,
at this time and for always,
his peace in your soul,
his presence in your heart,
and his power in your life.[12]

10. PRAYERS OF COMMENDATION

10a   A stillborn baby

Into your hands we put ourselves and all stillborn babies,
who were born not into life here
but born into your love,
the love that is waiting for us all.
Heavenly Father, we commend them to your love, and
entrust them to your tender and merciful care. Amen.[2]

10b   A child or baby

Into God's loving care and compassion, into the arms of
that infinite mercy, we commend (this baby) in the assurance that he/she will share in the risen life of Jesus Christ,
our Saviour.[17]

10c Babies and children

Dear God,
Jesus took children in his arms and blessed them:
into your strong and gentle hands
we entrust our precious children,
sheep of your fold,
lambs of your flock.
We believe that Jesus died and rose again to save us
and so we offer this prayer in his name.[2]

10d A stillborn or miscarried baby

Father, help us to entrust this baby N. to your never failing
care. We give back to you, our heavenly Father, what you
once gave to us; which was always yours and always will be.
We believe that we are united with N. in your unending
love, through Jesus Christ our Redeemer.[2]

10e A miscarried or stillborn baby

Let us commend this baby to the Lord's merciful keeping;
and let us pray with all our hearts for N. & N.
Even as they grieve at the loss of their (little) child
they entrust him/her to the loving embrace of God.[1]

10f A miscarried baby

Loving Father, it is your purpose to bring to completion all
that your hands have made. We commend now to your
safe keeping these miscarried babies remembered today,
born before their time had come. Perfect that which you
have begun and take into your care these lives that you
have given. Give comfort and hope to those whose sorrow
is sharp and whose sadness fills our hearts. Through the
resurrection of Christ our Lord. Amen.[2]

10g Children of any age

We give back to you, O God, those whom you gave us. You
did not lose them when you gave them to us, and we do not
lose them by their return to you. Your dear Son has taught

us that life is eternal and love cannot die, so that death is only a horizon and a horizon is only the limit of our sight.

Open our eyes to see more clearly and draw us close to you, that we may know that we are nearer to our loved ones who are with you. You have told us that you are preparing a place for us: prepare us also for that happy place, that where you are may we also be always.[18]

11. PRAYERS OF COMMITTAL

11a   Babies before and after birth

Lord God, ever caring and gentle,
We commit our babies to your love.
You formed these children in the womb;
you have known them by name before time began.
We shall treasure them in our hearts for ever.[19]

11b   Babies before and after birth

In confidence we commit our little ones, living and departed, and ourselves, to the Good Shepherd, who cares for his lambs. Our children's souls dwell in the house of tomorrow.[2]

11c   Funeral for stillbirth or miscarriage

To you, O Lord, we humbly entrust N., so precious in your sight, and we now commit his/her body to be cremated. Ashes to ashes, dust to dust, in the promised hope of the resurrection.[2]

11d   Funeral for stillbirth or miscarriage

We have now come to say our goodbyes to N.,
and as we have entrusted him/her into your hands,
we now commit his/her earthly body to the elements.
Ashes to ashes, dust to dust;
having our whole trust and confidence in the mercy of our Heavenly Father
and in the victory of his Son, Jesus Christ our Lord,

who died, was buried and rose again for us,
is alive and reigns for ever and ever. Amen.[1]

11e Miscarriage

Lord God,
ever caring and gentle,
we commit to your love this little one,
who brought joy to our lives for so short a time.
Enfold him/her in your eternal life.[1]

11f Babies before and after birth

God of life, death and eternity,
we thank you for the gift of these babies and children,
and for the blessing through tears they have brought us.
Help us now to entrust them to your unfailing care and
love.
Transform our grief into new hope, and bring us to the
fullness and completeness of joy beyond our imagining.[4]

11g Miscarriage

Lord God, we return baby N. to you. As N. & N. grieve at
the loss of their child, we entrust N. to your loving care.[3]

12. PRAYERS FOR THE FAMILY

12a For parents

We pray for parents
devastated by the loss of their baby.
Give them courage
and help them in their pain and grief.
May they all meet one day
in the joy and peace of your Kingdom.

We ask this through Christ our Lord. Amen.[1]

12b For parents

Almighty God, Our Father who knew through the sacrifice
of his own Son, the pain of being a parent, comfort these

parents who have suffered the loss of their child. Be there in the darkness of grief to support their faltering steps in the days ahead.[20]

12c For a mother

Listen, Lord,
a mother praying
low and quiet,
listen please.
Listen to what her tears are saying.
See her heart upon its knees;
lift the load
from her bowed shoulders
till she sees
and understands
you, who hold the worlds together,
hold her problems in your hands.[21]

12d For mothers

Lord Jesus, your mother Mary stood by when you were dying.
Be near to the mothers of these children.
Be to them a strong and loving friend.
Give them healing for hurt,
and hope in place of desperation,
for you alone can show us how
to triumph over death. Amen.[2]

12e For parents

Jesus our Saviour, comfort these parents with the great power of your love as they mourn the death of their baby. Give them patient faith in their time of darkness and help them to an understanding and knowledge of your will. Strengthen them in their faith, and help them to remember that you care for them, now and always.[13]

12f   For parents

God our Creator,
From whom all life comes,
comfort this family, grieving for the loss of their hoped-for
child.
Help them to find assurance
that with you nothing is wasted or incomplete,
and uphold them with your love,
through Jesus Christ our Saviour.[15]

12g   For parents

O Lord, whose ways are beyond our understanding,
listen to the prayers of your faithful people:
that these weighed down with grief at the loss of this little
child
may find reassurance in your infinite goodness.
We ask this through Jesus Christ our Lord,
who lives and reigns with you and the Holy Spirit. Amen.[1]

12h   For parents after neonatal or cot death

Creator and sustainer of all, past, present and future, hear
us as we remember those babies who die shortly after
birth.
Your Son Jesus Christ, through agony in a garden,
found strength to face, in the emptiness of the cross,
the feelings of being forsaken.
Fill the emptiness of bereavement with the fullness of your
resurrection life. Amen.[22]

12i   For childless parents

We pray for those who have no children of their own.
Please grant them patience and peace of mind, O Lord,
and the strength to spread their love throughout the world
for the benefit of children everywhere.[3]

12j   For all parents

O God, our Heavenly Father, we bring before you the

troubles of pregnancy:
The sorrow of the bereaved,
The helplessness of the weak,
The despondency of the weary,
The fearfulness of the troubled,
The despair of the barren,
The loneliness of the childless,
The exhaustion of miscarriage.

Draw near to them all, for the sake of Jesus Christ our Lord, and help them to know the healing strength that comes from faith in you.[23]

12k For parents after abortion for abnormality

Dear Lord, for those whose babies are so imperfect in the eyes of the world, who are beautiful in our eyes but whom the world cannot support, give us courage to listen, so that we can do what is best for our children, for our families and for ourselves. For the babies, who in your eyes are perfect and beloved, bless and receive their souls.

For our families, give us strength to bear the grief and incomprehension that comes with knowing that one of our family has left us so early.

Give strength to the medical and caring professions, who also grieve as they try to help us in our sadness. Guide us, Lord, through these very dark days and help us to see and accept your love that is always there for us.[24]

12l For a family

Eternal Spirit, Earth-maker, Pain-bearer, Life-giver,
Source of all that is and shall be, Father and Mother of us all,
Loving God in whom is heaven,
enfold this family with your grace.
May their home be a place of your presence,
your forgiveness and your freedom.
May your will be done in them and through them
this day and for ever. Amen.[15]

12m For a family

Most merciful God,
whose wisdom is beyond our understanding,
surround the family of N. with your love;
that they may not be overwhelmed by their loss
but have strength to meet the days to come.[1]

12n For the brothers and/or sisters of the baby

Lord God, in the midst of death you gave us life. Be with
N. & N., for they are missing their baby sister/brother N.,
and do not understand why he/she had to die. Help them
to know that nothing you make is worthless, and that N. is
with you and will be always. May they always remember N.
as a special person in their lives, and keep him/her in their
hearts always.[2]

12o For the baby's grandparents

Lord God, our heavenly Father, you have watched over
our human family through the ages. Watch over these
grandparents, who are mourning the loss of their precious
grandchild N., while they watch over their own dear child
N. in his/her pain and sorrow. Grant them the faith to
endure these dark days, and strengthen the bonds of this
family, through Christ our Lord.[2]

13. PRAYERS OF HEALING

13a A prayer of St Francis

Lord, make me an instrument of thy peace,
where there is hatred, let me sow love;
where there is doubt, faith;
where there is darkness, light;
and where there is sadness, joy.
O Divine Master, grant that
I may not so much seek
to be consoled, as to console;

to be understood as to understand;
to be loved as to love;
for it is in giving that we receive,
it is in pardoning that we are pardoned,
and it is in dying that we are born into eternal life.[25]

13b   The wounded healer

Loving Lord,
time can only heal
provided I'm willing to take time
to realise that I have within my human mystery
the seeds of becoming a wounded healer.
By taking my own brokenness on board
and living with, in and through it
I gradually notice new strengths developing.
By giving my own wounds an airing
And letting them have breathing space,
I'm slowly but surely making more room for others in their
woundedness.
By feeling my own powerlessness
I begin to let a power greater than myself
have room and scope to work in me.

Lord of my memory and my memories,
let me let you heal me. Amen.[26]

13c   For healing

O Jesus, hear our prayer! Heal our hearts and minds. O
Lord, please come to us and heal us to love again. Bind up
our broken hearts. Let us feel your loving touch, and bring
into our lives knowledge of your love.[17]

13d   For healing

God our heavenly Father, we are numb with sorrow, open
our hearts with the power of your love.

Jesus Lord, we are filled with pain, place your healing
hands upon us and heal our hurts.

Spirit of God, we are empty and sorrowful; fill us with your spirit and bring us strength, healing and peace.[3]

13e For healing

Father, Lord of tiny things,
you marked the sparrow's fall:
please take the burden of our grief,
bring healing to us all.

Comfort us and heal us
in the sorrow that we share,
take and keep our little ones
in your eternal care.[3]

14. LETTING GO

14a A child

God of all consolation,
searcher of mind and heart,
the faith of these parents is known to you.
Comfort them with the knowledge
that the child for whom they grieve
is entrusted now to your loving care.
We ask this through Christ our Lord. Amen.[1]

14b To a child

Knowing you only in stillness and in silence, yet remembering you by your name, may God grant that when we wake in his light, it may be your voice that calls our names, and your sweet touch that wakes us.[2]

14c A miscarried baby

Lord, God of all creation,
we bless and thank you for your tender care.
Receive this life you created in love
and comfort your faithful people in their time of loss
with the assurance of your unfailing mercy.
We ask this through Christ our Lord. Amen.[27]

14d Babies

Creator God, give us together the ability to release daily our beloved babies to your loving presence. Help us to integrate into our lives pain that is past, present and future, that, having been blessed by your great love in the tiny form of our babies, we may be a blessing to others.[4]

15. PRAYERS OF THANKFULNESS

15a For brief lives

Lord of all life,
Thank you for your prodigality,
for your work in creation,
for nourishing life in the womb,
for your love even in death.
Thank you for these brief lives
whom you gave us and have taken to yourself.
Thank you for the arms of your love, embracing us all in your family.
Thank you for your presence in our sorrow and your strength in our continuing lives.[28]

15b The presence of God with the child

Heavenly Father,
your love for all children
is strong and enduring.
We were not able to know our baby N. as we hoped.
Yet our baby was known to you.
In the midst of our sadness
We thank you that N. is with you now.[13]

16. FINAL PRAYERS

16a After a funeral

God of mercy,
in the mystery of your wisdom

you have drawn this child to yourself.
In the midst of our pain and sorrow
we acknowledge you as Lord of the living and the dead
and we search for our peace in your will.
In these final moments we stand together in prayer,
believing in your compassion and generous love.[19]

16b After a memorial service

God our heavenly Father, we thank you for sharing with
these parents your power of creation and for sending
these babies and children into our lives. As they are now
born into you, so may we be comforted by the promise of
unending life, and come in time to the fullness and completeness of your presence.[2]

16c After a service for several families

Let us not be afraid, let us stop being anxious, for God our
Redeemer and Saviour is with us. Let us pray that we may
let go of these children with confidence, knowing that they
are in the hands of the heavenly Father. Small though they
were, there was in them a divine spark which death cannot
extinguish. May they see the face of God in heaven.
Amen.[29]

16d After a family service

And now may God fill you with his peace, may he comfort
you in the presence of his Holy Spirit. May every tear you
shed, every word you share, every memory you treasure
bring you deeper healing.
And may you always know that your baby is safe in God's
eternal care.[30]

16e After a funeral service

God of all mercies, you make nothing in vain,
and love all you have made.
Comfort us in our grief,
and console us by the knowledge of your unfailing love;
through Jesus Christ our Lord. Amen.[31]

16f   After a funeral

Heavenly Father,
you alone can heal our broken hearts;
you alone can wipe away the tears
that well up inside us;
you alone can give us the peace we need;
you alone can strengthen us to carry on.
We ask you to be near those
whose time of joy has been turned into sadness.
Assure them that with you
nothing is wasted or incomplete,
and uphold them with your tender love.
Supported by your strength
may our love for one another
be deepened by the knowledge
of your love for us all.[32]

16g   After a funeral

Compassionate God,
soothe the hearts of N. & N.
and grant that, through the prayer of Mary,
who also grieved by the cross of her son,
you may enlighten their faith
give hope to their hearts
and peace to their lives.
Lord, grant mercy to all the members of this family
and comfort them with the hope
that one day we will all live with you,
with your Son Jesus Christ, and the Holy Spirit,
for ever and ever. Amen.[27]

17. BLESSINGS

17a   A solemn blessing

May God, who loves all he creates, strengthen you and
bless you with the resurrection of his Son.

May we who live be granted healing, and may all your children who have died be given eternal light, peace and joy. May the God of consolation bless you in every way and sustain you in hope all the days of your life.[33]

17b   A small group

May our renewing God,
Birth-giver, Pain-bearer and Spirit of Life,
fill you with peace, encompass you with love
and be your hope,
today and every day.[34]

17c   A funeral

May the God of all consolation
bring you comfort and peace,
in the name of the Father and of the Son,
and of the Holy Spirit. Amen.[1]

17d   A memorial service

The LORD bless you
   and keep you;
the LORD make his face shine upon you
   and be gracious to you;
the LORD turn his face towards you
   and give you his peace.
                    Numbers 6:24–26 (NIV)

17e   A small group

May Christ the Good Shepherd
enfold you with love,
fill you with peace
and lead you in hope,
this day and all your days.[15]

17f   A funeral

O Lord, help us to remember that you care for us, and that your will is our peace.
And may the Lord Jesus Christ be with you to defend you,

within you to keep you, before you to lead you and above you to bless you. Amen.[2]

17g Any service

May the blessing of God be your comfort,
May the Son of God bring you peace:
May the Spirit of God be your promise to nourish faith that is deep.
May the warmth of the life of God within you be for ever, your blessing to keep. Amen.[4]

———

And if you have faith, everything you ask for in prayer you will receive. MATTHEW 21:22 (JB)

12

Poetry and Prose Readings

*May the words of my mouth and the meditation of my heart
  be pleasing in your sight,
  O LORD, my Rock and my Redeemer.*
                              PSALM 19:14 (NIV)

Note: Where no source is given, this is because we have
found these readings in places where no source was given
or author acknowledged. We welcome any information
which would enable us to credit these readings in later
editions of this book.

R1 NOT OUT OF MIND

Why should I be out of mind because I am out of sight? I am
waiting for you for an interval, somewhere very near, just
around the corner. All is well. Death is nothing at all. I have
only slipped away into the next room. I am I and you are
you. Whatever we were to each other, that we are still.

Canon H. Scott Holland

R2 WHAT IS DYING?

I am standing on the sea shore. A ship sails to the morning
breeze and starts for the ocean. She is an object of beauty
and I stand watching her till at last she fades on the horizon, and someone at my side says, 'She is gone'. Gone

where? Gone from my sight, that is all; she is just as large in the masts, hull and spars as she was when I saw her, and just as able to bear her load of living freight to its destination.

The diminished size and total loss of sight is in me, not in her; and just at the moment when someone at my side says, 'She is gone' there are others who are watching her coming, and other voices take up a glad shout, 'There she comes!' – and that is dying.

Bishop Brent

R3   THE REAPER

I am the reaper
All things with heedful hook
Silent I gather.
Pale roses touched with the spring,
Tall corn in summer
Fruits rich with autumn, and frail winter blossoms,
Reaping, still reaping,
All things with heedful hook
Timely I gather.
I am the sower.
All the unbodied life
Runs through my seed-sheet.
Atom with atom wed,
Each quickening the other
Fall through my hands, ever changing, still changeless.
Ceaselessly sowing,
Life, incorruptible life
Flows from my seed-sheet.
Maker and breaker
I am the ebb and the flood
Here and hereafter.
Sped through the tangle and coil
Of infinite nature,
Viewless and soundless I fashion all being.
Taker and giver

I am the womb and the grave
The Now and the Ever.

W. E. Henley

R4 GIVE SORROW WORDS

☆ Give sorrow words. The grief that does not speak Whispers the o'erfraught heart and bids it break.

William Shakespeare

R5 A HALF-STITCHED SCAR

Time does not heal,
It makes a half-stitched scar
That can be broken and you feel
Grief as total as in its first hour.

Elizabeth Jennings

R6 THE VIA DOLOROSA

Do not make the mistake
of imagining that you
may go singing on the Via Dolorosa.
Neither may you
bear right or left
the way is confined
with little room for manoeuvre.

You will know exhaustion

kneeling often
trodden and rough
and scarred by many feet,
this way is our way
and may not be shunned

turned from
or avoided –
best to go quietly
with a dogged courage
knowing that
one thing is certain
there is an end.
And when you arrive
you will find that the hill is crowned
with a living tree;
stretching out
great branches
to give shelter
and manna there
and spring water.

Margaret Torrie

R7 LIFE WITHIN

To have known life within
Is to have known joy
And the freshness of beginnings;
To have life snatched away
Leaves me with hands outstretched
My arms open wide,
Feeling emptiness and space
Rather than the weight of my child,
With newborn warmth and silken hair.
My body,
So full of kicks and squirms one day,
Is barren and lifeless the next –
Stripped of its child,
That I never knew.
Yet I did know
And loved.

Judy Gordon Morrow

R8 FOR A CHILD BORN DEAD

What ceremony can we fit
You into now? If you had come
Out of a warm and noisy room
To this, there'd be an opposite
For us to know you by. We could
Imagine you in lively mood

And then look at the other side,
The mood drawn out of you, the breath
Defeated by the power of death.
But we have never seen you stride
Ambitiously the world we know
You could not come and yet you go.

But there is nothing now to mar
Your clear refusal of our world.
Not in our memories can we mould
You or distort your character.
Then all our consolation is
That grief can be as pure as this.

Elizabeth Jennings

R9 STILL BORN

I carried you in hope,
the long nine months of my term,
remembered that close hour when we made you,
often felt you kick and move
as slowly you grew within me,
wondered what you would look like
when your wet head emerged,
girl or boy, and at what glad moment
I should hear your birth cry,
and I welcoming you
with all you needed of warmth and food:

we had a home waiting for you.
After my strong labourings,
sweat cold on my limbs,
my small cries merging with the summer air
you came. You did not cry.
You did not breathe.
We had not expected this;
it seems your birth had no meaning, or had you rejected us?
They will say you did not live
register you as 'stillborn'.
But you lived for me all that time
in the dark chamber of my womb.
And when I think of you now,
Perfect in your little death
I know that for me you are born still.
I shall carry you for ever.
My child, you were always mine,
you are mine now.
Death and life are the same mysteries.

Leonard Clark

R10 A LETTER TO MY BABY

Dear little boy, you left us so suddenly: you died at the very moment of your birth, snatched away from us without warning, right on the threshold of the outside world.

Such a tragedy, such a terrible pain. We were expecting such joy. We never even got to look into your eyes or see you smile; never got to nurse you at the breast, or hear and comfort your cry. Never had the sweet delight of getting to know your sweet personality, though we could see a hint of it in your beautiful gentle face as you lay in our arms and we cuddled you and covered you with kisses.

You were so perfect, so healthy, so big, every cell of your body bursting with potential. You were so strong and active inside me, so vital and full of life and happy and loving in your own way.

What a tragedy for us that you were never able to express that life outside the womb, at least in this world. You never got to know our faces, play with your brother, grow in our care. But what a joy for you – where you are now you will never feel pain, only happiness.

I have prayed that Jesus will tell you how much we love you and how desperately we wanted you to stay here with us. My sweet baby, my little man, I love you so much. So much love was waiting here just for you. It will always be only yours, waiting in that sad and hollow place in my heart until we meet again. We will miss you always.

Natalia Ord

R11 LITTLE LIVES

Like the rest of life's tragedies
You went your way. . . .

(Forgotten amid life's decay,
Just one more tear to mop up and hide:
an occasional thought.)

But don't give too much light
To little dead bodies,
The cries in the night;
And echoing wards,
So those dreams take flight. . . .

Many years have gone by,
And my heart can't fight
A faint shaft of sunlight – the tunnel is bright!
Oh, could it be that those little lives might
Now dwell with their Father in Heaven's glorious light?

Now my tears can flow,
But this time I know:
Little lives are safe
Because He told me so.

Vivien Saunders

R12 TAKE MY NAME

So tiny and so beautiful
You have left a massive hole in my soul.
I will cherish you as I cherish
Your mother and your brother
As a gift from our Maker.
Take my name with you,
For today it is all I am able to give.

Graham Ord

R13 TWO PIERCED HANDS

I had a sorrow so deep
that human love could not penetrate
its deepest recesses.
I stumbled through the valley
of suffering in my mind,
down, down into the depths of the darkness.
And there in the tearless pain beyond pain
I saw the hands outstretched.
Two pierced hands –
that was all I could see –
two pierced hands held out to me.

I knew that my sorrow was shared
to the uttermost,
That I did not stand alone in the darkness,
That every part of my pain was understood.
Two loving hands –
that was all I could see –
Two loving hands held out to me.

I felt no lessening of pain.
The stark reality of sorrow was still there,
to be faced and lived with.
But I was not alone.

In healing silence
two pierced hands had held mine
in the depths of that darkness.
Two sharing hands –
that was all I had seen –
two strong hands held out to me.

Mary Hathaway

R14   THE LOST CHILD

She was not no one.

She had a given name,
a drawer of knitted things,
matched suits and sweaters,
a crib under the window
where the sun could look.

'Others will come,' they said,
'to take her place'
                    (and they did).

'Lucky,' they said, 'it happened now before . . .'
                    (and it was true).
Nine swelling months,
like a small greek goddess,
she ruled my moods,
talking in a morse code
of thumps and kicks.

But born still-born she was bustled faceless away
to save a mother's
grief.
Foolish to mourn for someone,
who was nearly no one,
and after five long years grieve
still
                    though less and less.

Possibility
is not fact.
What never came to be
never was.

(Though half the world's mourning
is for what never
was.)

Still, it was an error
not to take that tiny shrivelled body
in my arms,
not to touch that thin, clenched face.
A grieving without shape
is imageless.

Like a golden fish it swims
under the sea, surfacing
at will,
or like a dark moon peers
through the window of any season
or any mood.

A grief without shape
is endless.
It has no grave.

Paul Petrie

R15 THE GATE OF THE YEAR

I said to the man who stood at the gate of the year, 'Give
me a light that I may tread safely into the unknown'. And
he replied: 'Go out into the darkness and put your hand
into the hand of God. That shall be to you better than light
and safer than the known way.' So I went forth, and finding
the hand of God trod gladly into the night. And he led me
towards the hills and the breaking day in the lone east.

M. Louise Haskins

R16 A GAELIC PRAYER

As the rain hides the stars,
as the autumn mist hides the hills,
as the clouds veil the blue of the sky so the dark
happenings of my lot hide the shining of your face from me.

Yet if I may hold your hand in the darkness it is enough.
Since I know that though I may stumble in my going, you
do not fall.

Translated by Alistair Maclean

R17 THEY ARE NOT LOST

They are not lost, our dearest loves
Nor have they travelled far
Just stepped inside home's loveliest room
And left the door ajar.

Anonymous

R18 LOVING AND LOSING

He whom we love and lose is no longer where he was
before: he is now wherever we go.

St John Chrysostom

R19 TURN AGAIN TO LIFE

If I should die and leave you here a while
Be not like the others sore undone, who keep
Long vigils by the silent dust and weep.
For my sake turn again to life and smile
Nerving thy heart and trembling hand, to do
Something to comfort weaker hearts than thine.
Complete those dear unfinished tasks of mine

And I perchance may therein comfort you.

Mary Lee Hall

R20   THE PROPHET

Then a woman said, Speak to us of Joy and Sorrow.
And he answered:
Your joy is your sorrow unmasked.
And the selfsame well from which your laughter rises was oftentimes filled with your tears.
And how else can it be?
The deeper that sorrow carves into your being,
the more joy it can contain.
Is not the cup that holds your wine the very cup that was burned in the potter's oven?
And is not the lute that soothes your spirit the very wood that was hollowed with knives?
When you are joyous, look deep into your heart and you shall find it is only that which has given you sorrow that is giving you joy.
When you are sorrowful, look again in your heart, and you shall see that in truth you are weeping for that which has been your delight.

Kahlil Gibran

R21   PROMISES

God has not promised
Skies always blue,
Flower strewn pathways
all our lives through
God has not promised
Sun without rain
Joy without sorrow
Peace without pain.

But God has promised
Strength for the day
Rest for the labour
Light for the day
Grace for the trials
Help from above
Unfailing sympathy
Undying love.

Annie Johnson Flint

R22 JOY AND WOE

Man was made for joy and woe
And when this we rightly know
Through the world we safely go.
Joy and woe are woven fine.
A clothing for their soul divine,
Under every grief and pine
Runs a joy with silken twine.

William Blake

R23 HEAL US ALL

O Saviour Christ our woes dispel
for some are sick and some are sad;
and some have never loved you well,
and some have lost the love they had.
Your touch has still its ancient power
No word from you can fruitless fall:
Here in this joyful worship hour
and in your mercy, heal us all.

Henry Twells, a 19th-century prayer

R24 ON LOVE

In our creation we had a beginning, but the love in which

he created us was in him without beginning, and in his love we have our beginning. All this we shall see in God without end, which may Jesus grant us. Amen.

Mother Julian of Norwich

R25   A ROSE

Here lies a rose, a budding rose
Blasted before its bloom;
Whose innocence did sweets disclose
Beyond that flower's perfume.

To those who for her loss are grieved
This consolation given,
She's from a world of woe relieved
And blooms a rose in heaven.

Robert Burns

R26   PETALS

A flower has fallen into the water
Its petals spread wide to show their beauty to the world
It is caught by the falling tide
And carried to the ocean
Of our God.

Valerie Austin and Charles Clarke Smith

R27   THE UNFINISHEDS

We cannot judge a biography by its length, by the number of pages in it; we must judge by the richness of the contents. . . . Sometimes the 'unfinisheds' are among the most beautiful symphonies.

Victor Frankl

R28 HE LOVETH ALL

He prayeth best who loveth best
All things both great and small
For the dear God who loveth us
He made and loveth all.

Samuel Taylor Coleridge

R29 A LITTLE THING

Also in this revelation he showed a little thing,
the size of a hazelnut
in the palm of my hand
and it was as round as a ball.

I looked at it with my eye of understanding and thought:
what can this be?
And it was gently answered thus: 'It is all that is made.'

I marvelled how it could continue,
because it seemed to me it could suddenly have sunk into
nothingness
because of its littleness.

And I was answered in my understanding: 'It continueth
and always shall because God loveth it;
and this way everything hath its being by the love of God.'

In this thing I saw three characteristics:
the first is that God made it,
the second is that God loves it,
the third that God keeps it.

Mother Julian of Norwich

R30 STRONG IN LOVE

The strings of a harp are of many lengths. As God strikes
the note Humanity sings. The spirit is the harpist and all
the strings must sound which are strong in love.

Mechtild

R31   FOOTPRINTS ON MY HEART

Some people
come into our lives
and quickly go.
Some stay for a while
and leave footprints on our hearts,
and we are never,
ever the same.

From a special liturgy

R32   TO DAFFODILS

Fair daffodils, we weep to see
  You haste away so soon;
As yet the early-rising sun
  Has not attained his noon.
     Stay, stay,
   Until the hasting day
    Has run
   But to the evensong;
And, having prayed together, we
  Will go with you along.

We have short time to stay as you,
  We have as short a spring;
As quick a growth to meet decay,
  As you, or anything.
     We die,
   As your hours do, and dry
    Away
   Like to the summer's rain;
Or as the pearls of morning's dew,
  Ne'er to be found again.

Robert Herrick

R33   THE LILY OF THE DAY

It is not growing like a tree
In bulk does make men better be;
Or standing long as oak, three hundred years
To fall at last dry, bald and sere

A lily of a day
Is fairer far in May

Though it fall and die that night
It was the plant and flower of light
In small proportion we beauty see
And in short measure life may perfect be.

Ben Jonson

R34   THE SERENITY PRAYER

God, grant us the serenity
To accept what cannot be changed
The courage to change what can be changed
and the wisdom to know the difference.

Reinhold Niebuhr

R35   THE STILLBORN

(Two speakers)

We are the stillborn,
born from the dark into the dark:
We are the lost ones,
the world will never know our names.

(There is a memory
Of tiny fingers, white and limp.
There is a picture
Of a small, still, white bundle.)

We know a secret love –
our mothers nurse us in their hearts.
We know no memory
of breast or soft touch, cradling.

(There will be tears
When stark numbness thaws.
There is a silence –
A cot behind the yellow door.)

Our mothers hold us,
See us growing in their minds' eye:
Born between two worlds
We may not walk, or see: we may not fly.

(A yearning
When other people's babies romp:
Searching
For another child to hold.)

We were born to darkness
Yet there is a light above us we can see:
Our mothers love us,
We are ready to be born again and free.
There is a loving
That is strong and everlasting, true:
Now is the moment
To take that loving with us as into love we go.

Althea Hayton

=====

Worry makes a man's heart heavy, a kindly word makes it glad.
PROVERBS 12:25 (JB)

13

Useful Books

And I saw the dead, great and small, standing before the throne, and books were opened. Another book was opened, which is the book of life. REVELATION 20:12 (NIV)

Miscarriage

ALLEN, M. & MARKS, S. *Miscarriage: Women Sharing from the Heart* (Wiley, 1993)

FRIEDMAN, R. & GRADSTEIN, B. *Surviving Pregnancy Loss: a Complete Sourcebook for Women and their Families* (Citadel, 1992)

HEY, V. and others (eds.) *Hidden Loss: Miscarriage and Ectopic Pregnancy* (Women's Press, 1996)

KOHN, I. & MOFFITT, P. *Pregnancy Loss – Guidance and Support for You and your Family* (Headway, 1994)

KOHNER, N. & HENLEY, A. *When a Baby Dies: the Experience of Late Miscarriage, Stillbirth and Neonatal Death* (Pandora, 1995)

MURPHY, S. *Talking about Miscarriage* (Sheldon Press, 1992)

MOULDER, C. *Miscarriage* (Pandora Press, 1996)

OAKLEY, A. *Miscarriage* (Penguin, 1996)

The death of a baby

HAYTON, A. *Lucy's Baby Brother* (Wren Publications, P.O. Box 396, St Albans, AL3 6NE, 1995)

HILL, S. *Family* (Michael Joseph, 1989)

KOHNER, N. & HENLEY, A. *When a Baby Dies: the Experience of Late Miscarriage, Stillbirth and Neonatal Death* (Pandora, 1995)

PARKES, C. M. *Bereavement: Studies of Grief in Adult Life* (Pelican, 1980)

STICKNEY, D. *Water Bugs and Dragonflies* (Mowbray, 1982)

WOOD, A. (ed.) *Brief Lives: Parents Writing About the Death of a Baby* (National Childbirth Trust, 1995)

For professionals

ALDERSON, P. (ed.) *Saying Goodbye to your Baby* (SANDS, 1986)

BOURNE, S. & LEWIS, E. *Psychological Aspects of Stillbirth and Neonatal Death: An Annotated Bibliography* (Tavistock Clinic, 1992)

Bereaved Parents and the Professional. Leaflet available from The Compassionate Friends. (For address see p. 181.)

HUISJES, H. J. & LUND, T. (eds.) *Early Pregnancy Failure* (Churchill Livingstone, 1996)

KOHNER, N. *A Dignified Ending: Recommendations for Good Practice in the Disposal of Bodies and Remains of Babies Born Before the Legal Age of Liability* (SANDS, 1992)

Ministering to Bereaved Parents. Leaflet available from The Compassionate Friends. (For address see p. 181.)

Miscarriage, Stillbirth and Neonatal Death: Guidelines for Professionals (SANDS, 1991)

Grief

APPLEBAUM, A. (ed.) *Empty Arms: Coping After Miscarriage, Stillbirth and Infant Death* (Wintergreen, 1990)

BAUMAN, H. *Living through Grief* (Lion, 1994)

HAYTON, A. *The Silver Bird* (Wren Publications, P.O. Box 396, St Albans, AL3 6NE, 1997)

KANDER, J. *So I will Comfort You . . .* (Gracewing, 1990)

KRAYBILL, N. & KRAYBILL, E. *Miscarriage: a Quiet Grief* (Herald Press, 1992)

KUSHNER, H. *When Bad Things Happen to Good People* (Pan, 1982)

LEWIS, C. S. *A Grief Observed* (Faber and Faber, 1961)

MORROW, J. & De HAMER, N. *Good Mourning: Help and Understanding in Time of Pregnancy Loss* (Word, 1980)

NICHOL, M. *Loss of a Baby: Understanding Maternal Grief* (Bantam, 1989)

PINCUS, L. *Death and the Family* (Faber, 1981)

SCHIFF, H. S. *The Bereaved Parent* (Souvenir Press, 1979)

SHAWE, M. *Enduring, Sharing, Loving: for All Those Affected by the Death of a Child* (Darton, Longman and Todd, 1992)

TAYLOR, R. L. & WATSON, M. J. (eds.) *They Shall Not Hurt: Human Suffering And Human Caring* (Colorado Associated University Press, 1990)

WILKINSON, T. *The Death of a Child : a Book for Families* (Julia Macrae, 1991)

Liturgy

BENTLEY, J., BEST, A. & HUNT, J. *Funerals, a Guide: Prayers, Hymns and Readings* (Hodder and Stoughton, 1994)
Book of Commons (including an order for the funeral of a stillborn child) (St Andrew Press, Edinburgh)

COOPER, A. *It's Hard to Say Goodbye* (Bassetlaw Hospital, Kilton, Worksop, S81 0BD, 1996)

Funeral Services and Resources (The Anglican Church of Australia Trust Corp., 1993)

Funeral Service for a Child Dying Near the Time of Birth (Church House Publishing, 1989)

HAYTON, A. *Prayer After Abortion* (Wren Publications, P.O. Box 396, St Albans, AL3 6NE, 1997)

JAY, C. *A Celebration of Life – a Cathedral Liturgy* (Child Bereavement Trust, 1 Millside, Bourne End, Bucks, 1995)

McALL, K. *Healing the Family Tree* (Sheldon Books, 1984)

Order For the Naming and Commendation of an Infant who Died Before Birth (Office of Worship, Archdiocese of St Louis, 7800 Kerrick Road, St Louis, Miss. 63119, 1990)

Order of Christian Funerals (Geoffrey Chapman, 1991)

SMITH, N. *Miscarriage, Stillbirth and Neonatal Death: Guidelines in Pastoral Care for Clergy and Hospital Chaplains* (Committee for Hospital Chaplains, London, 1989)

The New Zealand Prayer Book, He Karakia Mihinare o Aotearoa (William Collins Publishers Ltd, P.O. Box 1, Auckland)

WALTER, Tony *Funerals and How to Improve Them* (Hodder and Stoughton, 1990)

WARD, H. & WILD, J. *Human Rites: Worship Resources for an Age of Change* (Mowbray, 1995)

Pastoral care

A Handbook on Hospital Chaplaincy (Hospital Chaplaincies Council, Church House, Great Smith Street, London SW1P 3NZ)

Pastoral Guidelines and a Funeral Service for Stillbirths and Death in Early Infancy (Church of Scotland, 1986)

WRETMARK, A. *Perinatal Death as a Pastoral Problem* (Almqvist International, P.O. Box 4627, S-11691 Stockholm, 1993)

Readings

WHITAKER, A. (ed.) *All in the End is Harvest: An anthology for Those who Grieve* (Darton, Longman and Todd, 1984)

Prayer

BATCHELOR, M. (Ed.) *The Lion Prayer Collection: over 1300 Prayers for All Occasions* (Lion, 1996)

BLACKLEDGE, D. *Loving Lord* (Sanctuary Books, 1 Winckley Square, Preston, Lancs)

BUTLER, C. *In This Very Hour: Loss of an Unborn Child: Devotions for Your Time of Need* (Broadman & Holman, 1994)

CARDEN, J. (ed.) *Morning Noon and Night* (Church Missionary Society, 1976)

GUEST, A. *A Little Book of Comfort* (Marshall Pickering, 1995)

HAYTON, A. *Prayer in Pregnancy* (Wren Publications, P.O. Box 396, St Albans, AL3 6NE, 1995)

LINN, M. and others *At Peace With The Unborn: a Book for Healing* (Paulist Press, 1993)

Poetry

HAINES, P. C. & HARRIS, L. *Angels of the Heart* (24 Rockcliffe Avenue, Bath, BA2 6QP, 1994)

JENNINGS, E. *Collected Poems* (Carcanet, 1980)

———

One last thing, my son, be warned that writing books involves endless hard work, and that too much study wearies the body.
ECCLESIASTES 12:12 (JB)

14

Helpful Organisations

The King will reply, 'I tell you the truth, whatever you did for one of the least of these brothers of mine, you did for me.' MATTHEW 25:40 (NIV)

UNITED KINGDOM

Alder Centre, Royal Liverpool Children's NHS Trust, Alder Hey, Eaton Road, Liverpool, L12 2AP
Tel: 0151 252 5391 (daytime)
Helpline: 0151 228 9759 (evenings)
Support and counselling for anyone affected by the death of a child.

British Infertility Counselling Association, 69 Division St., Sheffield, S1 4GE
Referral to counselling, promoting accessible counselling services for people with infertility problems. Training, workshops and study days. (Including childlessness due to repeated pregnancy loss.)

Blisslink Nippers, 17–21 Emerald St., London, WC1N 3QL
Tel: 0171 831 8996
Charity raising funds for special baby units. Also funds a support and information service for parents with babies on life support and in intensive care. Includes bereavement support.

Compassionate Friends (TCF), 53 North St., Bristol, BS3 1EW
Tel: 0117 966 5202
Helpline: 0117 953 9639
An international organisation of bereaved parents offering friendship and understanding to other bereaved parents.

Cot Death Society, 1 Browning Close, Thatcham, Newbury, RG18 3EF
Research and information for families after cot death, lending respiration monitors for subsequent babies.

The Child Bereavement Trust, 1 Millside, Riversdale, Bourne End, SL8 5EB
Providing support and information for bereaved parents and training resources for staff.

Christian Child Care Network, 10 Crescent Road, South Woodford, London, E18 1JB
Tel: 0181 559 1133
Counselling helpline for children and their families. Extensive database of Christian helping and caring agencies. Local helplines to become available (see local directories).

The Churches Committee For Hospital Chaplaincy, Church House, Great Smith St, London, SW1P 3NZ
Professional body for hospital chaplains.

College of Health Care Chaplains, P.O. Box 255, Canterbury, CT2 8AH
Training resources and *Hospital Chaplain*, a newsletter for health care chaplains of all denominations.

Cruse, Cruse House, 126 Sheen Road, Richmond, TW9 1VR
Tel: 0181 940 4818
Helpline: 0181 332 7227
Information and support on all aspects of bereavement. Local counselling for bereaved people.

Foundation for the Study of Infant Deaths, 14 Halkin St.,
London, SW1X 7DP
Tel: 0171 235 0965
Cot Death Helpline: 0171 235 1721
24-hour helpline, befrienders, advice and information for
parents and others experiencing sudden infant death.

Hospital Chaplaincy Council, Church House, Great
Smith St., London, SW1P 3NZ
Professional support for hospital chaplains and publica-
tions relating to chaplaincy issues.

**International Institute for Pregnancy Loss and Child
Abuse Research and Recovery (IIPLCARR),** Mrs P. Wil-
liamson, 24 Coleman Road, West Howe, Bournemouth
Tel: 01202 571072
Research, literature, professional support, group therapy
training for those affected by miscarriage and abortion.

ISSUE (National Fertility Association), 114 Lichfield St.,
Walsall, WS1 1SZ
Helpline: 01922 722888
Advice and information for people with infertility and
related problems.

Marriage and Family Life Commission, Christian Educa-
tion Centre, 4 Southgate Drive, Crawley, RH10 6RP
Tel: 01923 616945
Roman Catholic organisation. Arranges events centred
around spiritual issues surrounding marriage and family
life.

MIDIRS (Midwives Information and Resources Service),
Institute of Child Health, Royal Hospital for Sick Chil-
dren, St Michael's Hill, Bristol, BS2 8BJ
Tel: 0117 925 1791
An educational charity producing information packs dis-
tributed to midwives.

The Miscarriage Association, c/o Clayton Hospital, Northgate, Wakefield, WF1 3JS
Helpline: 01924 200799
Charity acknowledging pregnancy loss. Local support groups for parents bereaved by miscarriage. Newsletter. 24-hour helpline.

Multiple Births Foundation, Queen Charlotte's and Chelsea Hospitals, Goldhawk Road, London, W6 0XG
Tel: 0181 748 4666
Local support to parents of twins and triplets (and more). Advice and training materials for professionals working with them.

National Association of Bereavement Services, The Laura Centre, 4 Tower St., Leicester, LE1 6WS
Tel: 0171 247 1080
A charity promoting awareness of bereavement services with research and information for all those involved with bereavement. *Lifeline* magazine. Local support.

National Board of Catholic Women, 25 Richmond Park Road, London, SW14 8JU
Consultative body to the Bishops' Conference of England and Wales. Publishers of *Catholic Woman*.

Relate, Herbert Grey College, Little Church St., Rugby, CV21 3AP
Tel: see local directory.
Confidential counselling for relationships of any kind, including marital difficulties after the death of a child.

Remember Our Child, 50 University St., Belfast, BT7 1HB
Tel: 01232 333315
Partnership of child loss support groups in Northern Ireland.

St Gerard Family League, Alphonsus House, Chawton
Alton, Hants.
Tel: 01420 88222
An association of Christians united in prayer for their own
and other families. Newsletter and published prayers.

Share group UK, c/o Rev. Roy Bennett, Bassetlaw
Hospital, Kilton, Worksop, S81 0BD
Tel: 01909 500990
Resources for bereaved parents, caregivers and other
interested persons. Publications and information on
farewell rituals after pregnancy and infant loss.

**Society for Counselling and Information on Miscarriage
(SCIM),** 2nd Floor, 274 Bath St., Glasgow, G2 4GR
Tel: 0141 572 0105
Telephone and personal support for parents after miscar-
riage. Information and leaflets etc.

The Stillbirth And Neonatal Death Society (SANDS), 28
Portland Place, London, W1N 5DE
Tel: 0171 436 5881
Support for parents after a baby dies. Helpline and publi-
cations. Local support groups.

Support Around Termination For Abnormality (SATFA),
73 Charlotte St., London, W1P 1LB
Tel/fax: 0171 631 0280
Helpline: 0171 631 0285
Helping parents who discover that their baby is abnormal.
Telephone befriending before and after abortion and with
subsequent pregnancies. Newsletter and booklets.

Twins and Multiple Births Association (TAMBA), P.O.
Box 30, Little Sutton, South Wirral, L66 1TH
Tel: 0151 348 0020
Support groups for parents who have lost one or both
twins or babies from a multiple birth.

Women Hurt by Abortion, 42 Chessel Avenue, Bitterne, Southampton, SO19 4DX
Tel: 01703 394890
Support group, booklets.

IRELAND

Irish Miscarriage Association, 27 Kenilworth Road, Dublin 6
Tel: 01 972938
Information and support for families after miscarriage.

Irish Sudden Infant Death Association, c/o Carmichael Centre, North Brunswick St, Dublin 7
Support and information for parents after a cot death.

Stillbirth And Neonatal Death Society (SANDS), c/o Carmichael Centre, North Brunswick St., Dublin 7
Support, information and resources for families after stillbirth.

UNITED STATES OF AMERICA

Amend, c/o Martha Eise, 1559 Villa Rose, Hazelwood, MO 63042
Memorial booklet *Special Babies.*

Center for Loss in Multiple Birth (CLIMB), P.O. Box 1064, Palmer, AK 99645
Tel: 907–746–6123

The Compassionate Friends, National Headquarters, P.O. Box 3696, Oak Brook, IL 60522
Tel: 708–990–0010

Pregnancy And Infant Loss Centre, Suite 22, 1415 East Wayzata Blvd., Wayzata, MN 54601
Workshops, booklets.

Pregnancy and Infant Loss Support Inc. (SHARE), National SHARE office, St Joseph's Center, 300 First Capitol Drive, St Charles, MO 63301
Tel: 314 947 6164
Fax: 314 947 7486
Information and resources. Support groups for parents bereaved by pregnancy loss. Book about baby memorial services. Video for bereaved siblings in English and Spanish.

Reach Out to the Parents of an Unknown Child Inc., 55 North Country Road, St James, NY 11780
Tel: 516 862 6743 or 516 584 5525

Resolve Inc. (Infertility), National office, 1310 Broadway, Somerville, MA 02144
Tel: 617–623–0744

CANADA

Compassionate Friends (National Office), 685 William Avenue, Winnipeg, Manitoba R3E 0Z2
An international organisation of bereaved parents offering friendship and understanding to other bereaved parents.

International Institute for Pregnancy Loss and Child Abuse Research and Recovery (IIPLCARR), P.O. Box 27103, Colwood Corners, Victoria, BC. V9B 5S4
Tel: 604–391–1840
Workshops, therapy groups, research and publications for professionals and parents after pregnancy loss, including abortion.

Perinatal Bereavement Services of Ontario, 60 Church St., Markham, Ont. L3P 2L9
Tel: 905 472 1807
Meetings, telephone help, resources and books.

AUSTRALIA

Barwon Paediatric Bereavement Program, P.O. Box 281, Geelong, Victoria 3220
Tel: 03 5226 7525
A support and information programme for bereaved parents in rural Victoria.

Compassionate Friends (TCF)

TCF New South Wales
115 Pitt St, Sydney, New South Wales 2000
Tel: 02 9233 3731
Freecall: 1800 671 621

TCF Queensland
P.O. Box 218, Springwood, Brisbane, Queensland 4127
Tel: 07 3279 1960

TCF Victoria
Bereaved Parents Centre, 300 Camberwell Road, Camberwell, Melbourne, 3124
Tel: 03 9882 3355
Freecall: 1800 641 091

TCF Western Australia
79 Stirling Street, Perth 6000
Tel: 09 277 5698

TCF South Australia
P.O. Box 93, Parkhome 5043
Tel: 08 351 0344

TCF Tasmania
P.O. Box 1357P, Hobart 7000
Tel: 03 6243 9665

Support groups, information, counselling, resources, for parents bereaved by the loss of a baby or child.

Sisters of Charity Outreach Centre, 72 Fitzroy St, Fitzroy, Victoria 3065
Tel: 03 9415 1522
Grief counselling and support.

Stillbirth And Neonatal Death Support (SANDS), c/o 19 Canterbury Road, Canterbury, Victoria 3124
Information and group support for families after stillbirth.

Sudden Infant Death Research Foundation, 1227 Malvern Road, Malvern 3144
Tel: 03 9822 9611
Research and support for families after cot death.

═══

Then Peter addressed them: 'The truth I have now come to realise' he said 'is that God does not have favourites, but that anybody of any nationality who fears God and does what is right is acceptable to him.' ACTS 10:34–5 (JB)

15

Epilogue

This book is not intended to be an answer to the dilemma of meeting the pastoral needs of bereaved parents while maintaining the traditional practices of the Christian church, hospitals and funeral services. Yet I believe that society has the power to make sure that these practices are changed – and I know that the power we need lies in the hearts and minds of bereaved parents themselves.

The death of a baby runs counter to the forces of nature. A woman in labour has mustered all her powers of creative energy to work in the delivery. She is at her most vulnerable, for she may die, yet she is also at her most powerful.

The creative urges associated with the nurture and birth of her new child are hormonally based and genetically programmed. They are built into her very being. If the baby loses its chance of life, the woman loses her power to bring this new life to birth. This is the true tragedy. The mother is suddenly rendered powerless, impotent and angry. Her power has been wrenched from her by this death.

For far too long, society has chosen to render this mother more impotent by denying her any access to the reality of her child, upon whom all her being has been focused for many weeks. Today, society is reluctantly allowing her the opportunity to express her creative energies after the death of her baby in order to bring about her own healing. The former strategy of 'out of sight, out of mind' is now seen as callous, and rightly so.

The conception of a baby re-enacts the power of God in

creation, yet within the human body. The energy that this generates fills the womb and all that is within it, and spreads to the family and the society within which the woman lives. Everyone is filled with new hope and faith when a new baby is on the way. When the life of the baby ends, so early that the world may never know it, there remains the hope and freshness of renewal that the baby brought to the world during its short life. There also remains the mother's residual creative energy, yearning for a chance to be expressed.

I believe that we should seek to harness this untapped well of creative energy – the hidden grief of bereaved parents. As we bring this grief to the surface, we will begin to see the renewing power of that energy.

The female side of God

We have a masculine faith, expressed in male ways, which has managed to survive the centuries, but today does not include much of the female side of spirituality. Women are spiritual beings, more or less because they have the capacity to share so intimately in the act of creation. Church congregations are predominately female for this reason.

Liturgy for pregnancy loss necessarily emphasises the female aspects of the power and love of God. Within these liturgies lie the first glimmerings of a new theology of pregnancy and birth, which I believe will change for ever our view of the conception and birth of a child.

Women speak out

What changes there may be, might be seen reflected in the attitude of Jesus to a woman with a very similar problem. Luke, physician that he was, saw how Jesus gave help to a woman in despair, but also enabled her to help herself.

> Now there was a woman suffering from a haemor-rhage for twelve years, whom no one had been able to cure. She came up behind him and touched the fringe of his cloak; and the haemorrhage stopped at

that instant. Jesus said, 'Who touched me?' When they all denied that they had, Peter and his companions said, 'Master, it is the crowds round you, pushing.' But Jesus said, 'Somebody touched me. I felt that power had gone out from me.' Seeing herself discovered, the woman came forward trembling, and falling at his feet, explained in front of all the people why she had touched him and how she had been cured at that very moment. 'My daughter,' he said, 'your faith has restored you to health; go in peace.' Luke 8:43–8 (JB)

There is much in this story to help us understand how we as Christians, as followers of Jesus, should react to parents after pregnancy loss.

We have to remember that, according to the law of Moses, the woman would have been unclean for twelve years, and was therefore denied the spiritual comfort of the temple. Here is a parallel with miscarrying women, denied access to services of prayer and pastoral support.

The woman knew that the slightest contact with Jesus was all she needed to bring relief. She did not touch his body, lest she make him unclean too; she only needed to touch the hem of his garment. In the same way, bereaved parents need only to know that, if they too reach out, their need will be recognised in the very moment of their despair.

Yet this was not a small and private thing between the woman and Jesus, as it perhaps should have been, dealing as it did with a very personal problem. Jesus insisted that he should know how his power had been used. The woman, until then an outcast, had to overcome her shyness and publicly announce the reason for her distress.

The message in this story is that, however private the problem may be, men and women should not be afraid to openly reach out for Jesus. Bereaved parents can, and must, announce their need to the world. Then, like the trembling woman Luke describes, faith will bring them healing and they will find peace.

16

References

1: Baptism and its alternatives

1 The Senior Chaplain, Musgrove Park Hospital, Taunton, Somerset. Unpublished letter used with permission of the author.

2 I am grateful to a vicar in Wales for his honest observations on this point.

3 An observation made to me in 1993 in a letter from a senior chaplain in Witchita, Kansas.

4 This section and model liturgy are based upon suggestions made by the Chaplaincy team at Musgrove Park Hospital (see ref 1).

5 From a special liturgy sheet.

6 I am grateful to my husband John, an Anglican priest, for this prayer, used with his permission.

7 These words are taken from a blessing and naming card, made for a family by the Bradford Mothers' Union, Yorks, in 1994.

8 This service was written by Bishop Peter Firth. Reproduced with his permission.

2: Baby Funerals

1 For more detail on this point, see Simon Knowles, 'A passage through grief – the Western Rural Pregnancy Loss team'. *British Medical Journal* 1994 (309), p. 1706.

2 Mrs C. Jay of Guildford SANDS. Some personal reflections on the funeral for her baby Laura in 1987, used with her permission.

3 'Mourning made easier if parents can view the body of neonate,' *Obstetric and Gynaecology News* 11:21, p. 35.

4 Funerals for babies and children have a certain sameness, as they tend to be drawn from the same limited range of printed resources. It is for this reason, among many others, that this book exists.

5 *Miscarriage, Stillbirth and Neonatal Death: Guidelines for Professionals* (SANDS, 1991) has completely altered attitudes to miscarriage and stillbirth in hospital in the UK.

6 I am grateful to the Ord family of St Albans, who have allowed extracts from the funeral service leaflet for their stillborn baby Josiah to be used as a resource for this project.

7 *A Celebration of Life*. Mrs Jay's idea for a memorial service came several years after an unsatisfactory funeral service for her stillborn baby Laura.

8 *Not Out of Mind Conference Report* (Wren Publications, 1994). A couple found that a Christian hospital administrator was the only person openly to share in their feelings of loss after their baby was stillborn in 1973 in Yorkshire.

9 A hospital pathologist carrying out autopsies on foetuses told me how he had to harden his heart in order to do his job: 'They expect us to think about them as babies, but they know what we have to do to them.'

10 The Child Bereavement Trust provides special staff training on this issue (see p. 181).

11 This section was prepared with the help of the Ord family (see ref 6).

12 This liturgy was created with the help of Rev. M. Crowther-Green, a vicar in Reading.

13 This story was told at the first Not Out of Mind conference by the mother of the child. In a real sense, her tiny son Joseph had come to give a silent testimony of his life and value.

14 Private communication with the editor.

15 For further details on this issue see *A Dignified Ending* (SANDS, 1992).

16 S. Bourne and E. Lewis, 'Perinatal bereavement: a milestone and some new dangers.' *British Medical Journal* 302 (18 May 1991), pp. 1167–8.

17 The Order of Christian Funerals 'Prayer for Parents who have Suffered Miscarriage' expresses the hope that all dead babies and their parents will be reunited one day in the peace and joy of the Kingdom of God.

18 Jenni Thomas, now Director of the Child Bereavement Trust, assures staff that suggesting the possibility of a funeral is not going to offend parents by implying that they have killed their child. 'The parents have been

through that, hundreds of times. These suggestions can't make it worse.' *Nursing Times*, 87:29 (17th July 1991), p.17.

19 SATFA newsletters, London, 1993–5. The readers' letters often display very strong and ambivalent feelings about a previous abortion for abnormality.

20 Noreen Riols' book *Abortion – a mother's birthright?* (Hodder, 1986), about her own experiences of abortion, describes the dawning realisation of loss after a period of denial.

21 In 1979 it was considered that including a prayer for after abortion in the official literature would be seen 'as giving a much more widespread approval to abortion than we would really be intending by including such a prayer.' Report of General Synod, Initiation services – series 3 (7th November 1979), p. 910.

22 This is only done in an informal way: to date I have not seen any special prayers for after abortion in any prayer book of any tradition of the Christian church.

3: Alternative Rites of Committal

1 In 1990 in the UK, SANDS carried out a questionnaire survey of hospital practice in the disposal of babies dying before 28 weeks of pregnancy. (This was the limit of viability at that time.) In some hospitals the pathologists routinely placed all pre-28-week babies sent for dissection in the waste disposal unit. The situation today is quite different, and miscarried babies are routinely shown to their parents. Pathologists have learned to repair foetuses given to them for dissection, so the parents can see them.

2 The Child Bereavement Trust (see page 181) is concerned with training nursing staff to deal sympathetically with this problem.

3 Creating a 'Dignified Disposal Policy' requires good

communication between the various departments of a hospital: the maternity wing, gynaecology, pathology, chaplaincy etc. Nonetheless, there are now many hospitals in the UK with such a policy.

4   This liturgy was compiled with the help of the Chaplain of St Mary's Hospital, London.

5   This liturgy is almost entirely taken from a printed service sheet depicting a service for the interment of ashes, written by Rev. Robert Anderson, chaplain of the King Edward Memorial Hospital, Western Australia, as a resource for the hospital. Used with permission.

6   A woman wrote to me to tell me that she attended a baby memorial service with her mother, only to find her mother crying for a baby sister she never knew she had.

7   This task may fall to the grandmother of the child, who is likely to be called upon at this time.

8   'How in the first numbness of your shock and grief can you *begin* to show or share what it feels like to crouch over the WC saying goodbye to the life you have conceived and carried within you, before flushing the remains of that passionately loved life away into the public sewers?' Private communication, 1993.

9   Some early ultrasonic scans reveal the fact that the amniotic sac is empty, or there is no developing baby there at all, despite a previous positive pregnancy test.

10 'Women's experiences of miscarriage in early pregnancy.' *Journal of Nurse-midwifery* 37:2 (Mar-Apr 1992), pp. 845–90.

11 In the UK, the public health regulations surrounding burial in the garden only apply to viable foetuses.

12 By the mid-1990s, almost all the new editions of Christian common prayer books had included a specially

adapted funeral service for a baby dying near the time of birth. (See Chapter 13.)

13 Before 1927, in the UK stillborn babies were not legally registered. It was common for babies to be named some time after birth, usually at baptism, and they were called 'baby' until that date. If they died before baptism, they were never named.

14 SANDS UK produced a special leaflet in 1993 that outlines how a baby's grave can be traced. This was published in response to an increasing demand for information.

15 For details of how to create a memorial see Chapter 8.

16 From an unpublished article: 'Memorial services for babies buried without a funeral', written by Rev. Mike Kavanagh and Sr Jayne Shepherd of Westwood Maternity Unit, Beverley, Yorks.

4: Prayer and Healing

1 This introduction and model liturgy was created (with a few additions) by Rev. Robert Anderson, Chaplain, King Edward Memorial Hospital for Women, Western Australia. Used with permission.

2 From *The Meditations of St Anselm* (Penguin, 1973), p. 154.

3 Harriet Goldenberg, 'The place of ritual as a marker of infertility.' *Journal of Fertility Counselling* 4:1 (Winter 1997).

4 Private communication.

5 Compiled with the help of Ms Meredith Wheeler of the British Infertility Counselling Association and Mrs Cox, a teacher from Worcestershire.

6 Adapted from a prayer of committal in a special memorial service booklet, Glasgow.

7   These ideas can be found in *Prayer After Abortion* (Wren Publications, 1997).

8   Adapted from a prayer for after abortion in *Prayer in Pregnancy* (Wren Publications, 1996).

9   This prayer was created by a Christian counsellor for the special conference.

10 This prayer was written by Bishop Peter Firth in 1979.

5: Baby Memorial Services for Small Groups

1   I am indebted to the Zambri family of Toronto, Canada, who kindly sent me details of a service they had held in memory of their baby Stéphanie who was stillborn in 1992. This service is now being used by other bereaved families and Catholic clergy in Ontario, Canada.

2   For an example of how a four-year-old sister may be involved in the death of her brother at birth, see Althea Hayton, *Lucy's Baby Brother* (Wren Publications, 1995).

3   Prayer composed by Onofri Zambri, father of Stéphanie (see ref 1). Used with permission.

4   Adapted from a spoken text within a song 'Peace is flowing like a river,' adapted by Rev. Carey Landry and published by Oregon Catholic Press, P.O. Box 18030, Portland, Oregon 97218–0030.

5   This liturgy is based on one created by Fr. Philip Law of Knebworth, and Rev. Diana Williams, of Potters Bar, and enacted as part of the 1994 Not Out of Mind conference.

6: Baby Memorial Services for Churches and Cathedrals

1   Dr James le Fanu wrote in *The Times* on 26th May 1994 ('When life never has a chance') that tender loving care had as much effect on the possibility of a live birth after repeated miscarriage as any other treatment.

2   It is likely that some women have attended baby

memorial services after an abortion, but have just kept quiet about it.

3   A vicar in Sheffield told me that their regular memorial services (at which they remember all those who have died recently or have anniversaries) attract 100–200 people, most of whom are not normally churchgoers.

4   In 1994 I attended a service in Guildford Cathedral. Much of the material in this chapter arises out of that experience.

5   These practical hints are taken from *A Celebration of Life* (Child Bereavement Trust, 1995).

6   I have been given liturgies from various cathedral services that have taken place around the United Kingdom. In almost every case surprisingly large numbers attended.

7   Caroline Jay, *A Celebration of Life*.

7: Special Eucharists

1   For a full background explanation of the use of this service see *Healing the Family Tree* by Dr Kenneth McAll (Sheldon, 1984).

2   *Healing the Family Tree*, p. 121.

3   *Ibid.*, p. 124.

4   I approached the parish priest of my local Roman Catholic church in 1991 about a Mass for parents after miscarriage. He told me that they had offered Mass regularly for some years but so few came it was no longer considered worth continuing.

5   *Liturgy* 12:6 (Aug/Sept 1988).

6   Francis Blodwell, 'Being church'. *Justpeace*, Journal of Pax Christi, 127 (Dec 1987), p. 1.

7   A parish priest in Knebworth, England, celebrated a

special Mass for 'All God's little ones' for the first time in his church in 1993. This is now a popular annual event.

8: Places and Times

1 Dr Colin Murray Parkes' work with widows in London in the 1970s laid the basis for our present understanding of bereavement. He introduced the idea of grief as a process, with certain definable stages.

2 From a talk about the grief of miscarriage at the first Not Out of Mind conference 1993.

3 I know of a woman who had six miscarriages and was regularly awakened by the imagined sound of babies crying, and found herself getting out of bed to calm them.

4 Details of how such a garden can be created can be obtained from the Child Bereavement Trust, England (see page 181).

5 In a side chapel of St Wilfrid's Church, Preston, Lancashire, is a wooden sculpture carved by Fenwick Lawson. It is a seated mother, seen as the universal mother, receiving, protecting and tenderly nestling the lost child in her hands by her left breast. Her eyes are closed to express an inner emotion, which leaves room for each individual to let her/his personal emotions flow freely. This forms the basis for a shrine for bereaved parents to visit and pray for their baby.

6 An exhibition of carved wooden female figures by Jean Lamb was held in Winchester Cathedral, England in 1994. One figure was exactly as described.

7 The Miscarriage Association in the UK asks members to send labels with the name of their baby to them each Christmas. These are all tied to a tree and make a moving testimony to the number of miscarried babies lost and mourned for.

8 Marie Jennings, 'Was I led or was I pushed?' *The Catholic Mother in Wales* (Mar 1995). Mrs Jennings was drawn quite suddenly and unexpectedly to a knowledge that St Jane Francis de Chantal might provide a focus for prayer for mothers after the death of a baby.

10: Music

1 Written for a special service at Walgrave Hospital, Coventry, in 1991. Published anonymously in *Hospital Chaplain* (Sep 1991). Reproduced by permission of author.

2 From 'Love from below', copyright Wild Goose Resource Group, Iona Community, Glasgow, G51 3UU. Reproduced by permission of the publishers in UK and also GIA Publications Inc., 7404 South Mason Avenue, Chicago, IL 60638, USA.

11: Further Prayers

(*Note:* For this section the editor has obtained sample liturgies from a variety of sources, and it has not been possible to ascertain the copyright source for every quotation. We welcome any information that will help us to acknowledge correctly the copyright holders in subsequent editions of this book.)

1 Original text and English translation from *Order of Christian Funerals* (Geoffrey Chapman, 1991) copyright © 1985, International Commission on English in the Liturgy, Inc. All rights reserved.

2 From a special liturgy service sheet.

3 Written by Althea Hayton.

4 Written by Rev. Robert Anderson. A resource for the King Edward Memorial Hospital for Women, 374 Bagot Road, Subiaco, Western Australia 6008. Used with permission.

5 Adapted from 'Funeral of a still-born child,' Common

Order, 1994. Copyright © Panel on Worship, Church of Scotland. Reproduced with permission.

6 Prayer from a funeral liturgy written by Rev. Crowther-Green, a vicar in Reading, England. Used with permission.

7 A prayer by Frank Colquhoun, from *The SPCK Book of Christian Prayer* (SPCK, 1995). Used with permission.

8 Adapted from a prayer by Henry Alford, found on the altar at Rome in the 19th century. From *Prayer across the Centuries* (Harold Shaw, 1993). Used by permission of Harold Shaw Publishers, Wheaton, IL 60189, USA.

9 A prayer by Betty Curti, quoted by Corrie ten Boom in *Jesus is Victor*, copyright © Fleming H. Revell, a division of Baker Book House, Grand Rapids, Michigan, USA. Used by permission of Kingsway Publications, Eastbourne.

10 Adapted from 'Trusting you, Lord' by Anne, in *Prayer in Pregnancy* (Wren Publications, 1996).

11 Adapted from a prayer by Rabbi Walter Rothschild, published in the *Miscarriage Association Newsletter*. 1993.

12 Written by Bernadette Zambri, mother of Stéphanie, stillborn in 1992 in Toronto, Canada. Used with permission.

13 Adapted from a prayer in *Funeral Services and Resources* (Anglican Church of Australia Trust, 1993).

14 Adapted from a 'Grandmother's prayer' in *Prayer in Pregnancy* (Wren Publications, 1996).

15 This copyright material is taken from *A New Zealand Prayer Book – he Karakia Mihinare o Aotearoa* and is used by permission.

16 Written by a Christian doctor working in general practice, and used with permission.

17 Part of a prayer composed during the Prayer After Abortion Conference, 1996, by one of those present.

18 William Penn (1644–1718).

19 Adapted from a prayer in *Order of Christian Funerals* (Geoffrey Chapman, 1991).

20 From a prayer by Diane Edwards (unpublished) with permission of the author.

21 Prayer by Ruth Bell Graham from *Prayer across the Centuries* (Harold Shaw, 1993). Used by permission of Harold Shaw Publishers, Wheaton, IL 60189, USA.

22 A prayer by Ted Burge, in *Lord of All, Hear Our Prayer* (Canterbury Press, 1992). Used with permission.

23 Adapted from a prayer by St Anselm.

24 Prayer by Elizabeth from *Prayer in Pregnancy* (Wren Publications, 1996). Used with permission.

25 The prayer of St Francis.

26 Extract from a prayer by Rev. Fr. Dennis Blackedge sj. In *Loving Lord – Horizons* (Sanctuary Books & Macmillan Nurses' Fund, 1 Winckley Square, Preston, PR1 3JJ, 1992). Used with permission of the author.

27 From 'Order for the blessing of parents after a miscarriage,' from *The Book of Blessings* (Catholic Book Co.).

28 Adapted from a prayer written by a couple whose baby had died. From *A Funeral service for a child dying near the time of birth* (Church House Publishing, 1989).

29 Adapted from a prayer by Rev. Robert Anderson (see ref 4).

30 From the Not out of Mind conference report (Wren Publications, 1994).

31 This extract from *Funeral service for a child dying near the time of birth* is copyright © the Central Board of

Finance of the Church of England 1989 and is reproduced by permission.

32 This extract from 'Funeral of a still-born child' is taken from Common Order, 1994, copyright © Panel on Worship, Church of Scotland, and is used with permission of the publishers.

33 From 'Celebrating brief lives,' *Liturgy* 12:6.

34 The final blessing from 'A funeral service for a child of God', by Rev. Robert Anderson (see ref 4) used with permission.

12: Poetry and Prose Readings

R1 Attributed to Canon H. Scott Holland. Source unknown.

R2 Bishop Brent. Source unknown.

R3 From 'Echoes' by W. E. Henley (1849–1903).

R4 From *Macbeth*, by William Shakespeare.

R5 From *Collected Poems* by Elizabeth Jennings (Macmillan, 1967). With permission of David Higham Associates.

R6 From *Poems for Those who Grieve* by Margaret Torrie/ CRUSE. Used with permission of the author's family.

R7 From *Good Mourning* by Judy Gordon Morrow and Nancy Gordon Word, 1989. Republished as *Silent Cradle* (Light and Life, 1997). Used with permission of the author.

R8 Poem from *Collected Poems* by Elizabeth Jennings (Macmillan, 1967). With permission of David Higham Associates.

R9 Poem from *The Way It Was* by Leonard Clark (Enitharmon Press, 1980). Permission given by the estate of Leonard Clark.

R10 Written by Natalia Ord, from funeral service leaflet for her son Graham Josiah, stillborn 19.7.94. With permission of the family.

R11 From 'Little Lives', an unpublished poem by Vivien Saunders. By permission of the author.

R12 Written by Graham Ord, from funeral service leaflet for his son Graham Josiah, stillborn, 19.7.94. With permission of the family.

R13 © Mary Hathaway. From *Hope for When I'm Hurting* (Lion Books, 1987). Reproduced by permission of the author.

R14 Poem by Paul Petrie first published 1984 in *Commonweal* (15 Dutch Street, NY 10038). Reproduced by permission of the editor.

R15 Part of 'The gate of the year' by M. Louise Haskins. Used with permission of the author's family.

R16 An ancient Celtic prayer translated by Alistair Maclean, from *The Lion Prayer Collection* (Lion, 1992).

R17 Anonymous.

R18 Prayer by St John Chrysostom.

R19 Poem by Mary Lee Hall, from *Bestloved Poems in Large Print* (G. K. Hall, 1983).

R20 Extract from *The Prophet* by Kahlil Gibran.

R21 'What God hath promised!' by Annie Johnson Flint (1866–1931).

R22 Poem from 'Auguries of innocence' by William Blake.

R23 Prayer by Henry Twells from *Prayer across the Centuries* (Harold Shaw, 1993) with permission of Harold Shaw Publishers, Wheaton, IL 60189, USA.

R24 From *A Lesson of Love*. Copyright 1988 by Fr. John-Julian OJN. Reprinted with permission from Walker

R25 Poem by Robert Burns.

R26 Extract from 'Beyond Death: A personal response', by Rex Bloomfield, in *Widowed What Now?* edited by Valerie Austin and Charles Clarke Smith (Mallison Rendel Publishers Ltd., Wellington, NZ). With permission.

R27 Extract From *Man's Search for Meaning* by Victor E. Frankl. Copyright © 1959, 1960, 1984, by Victor E. Frankl. Reproduced by permission of Hodder and Stoughton Ltd. UK and Beacon Press, USA.

R28 Extract from 'The Rime of the Ancient Mariner', Part VII, by Samuel Taylor Coleridge.

R29 Extract from *A Lesson of Love: the Writings of Mother Julian of Norwich,* translated by Fr. John-Julian OJN (Darton, Longman and Todd, 1988). Reproduced with permission of Walker & Company, New York, USA.

R30 Words by Mechtild, 13th-century mystic, an extract from his writings given to me in a private letter from the USA.

R31 Words taken from a liturgy service sheet, reprinted in *Hospital Chaplain* magazine (September 1991). Reproduced by permission of the editor.

R32 Poem by Robert Herrick.

R33 From a poem entitled 'To the immortal memory and friendship of that Noble pair Sir Lucius Cary and Sir Henry Morison' by Ben Jonson.

R34 Prayer by Reinhold Niebuhr, 1943. Reproduced by permission of the author's family.

R35 Poem by Althea Hayton, based on an idea from a SANDS group.